DRUMSET
& PERCUSSION RHYTHMS
FROM AROUND THE WORLD

180+ BEATS & PATTERNS
PLUS TUNING TIPS
RUDIMENTS & MORE

Project Editors: Felipe Orozco and Terry Silverlight

ISBN 978-1-5400-6065-5

Visit Hal Leonard Online at **www.halleonard.com**

Explore the entire family of Hal Leonard products and resources

World headquarters, contact:
Hal Leonard
7777 West Bluemound Road
Milwaukee, WI 53213
Email: info@halleonard.com

In Europe, contact:
Hal Leonard Europe Limited
Dettingen Way
Bury St. Edmunds, Suffolk, IP33 3YB
Email: info@halleonardeurope.com

In Australia, contact:
Hal Leonard Australia Pty. Ltd.
4 Lentara Court
Cheltenham, Victoria, 3192 Australia
Email: info@halleonard.com.au

CONTENTS

INTRODUCTION

This book is a reference guide for all percussion players, drummers, and rhythm enthusiasts. It provides thorough access to the most popular and influential rhythms from around the globe. Rhythms are ready and available for both beginner and advanced players alike. Strong knowledge of these rhythms will add to your resources and consequently broaden your knowledge in different styles.

While it is hard to outline the authenticity of all the rhythms presented in this guide due to the complexity of each style and the many variations of each rhythm, this book offers common and practical ways to play the most popular and influential rhythms from around the world.

The rhythms in this book are not transcriptions of actual performances and are meant to be used for educational purposes only.

How to Use This Book

It is strongly recommended that you develop a practice regimen in which you devote some time to learn each rhythm. Play each rhythm several times until you can master the "groove" of each one. Use a metronome and practice at several tempos until you are able to play each rhythm at different speeds.

Format

Each rhythm is written in either standard drumset or percussion notation (some rhythms have both percussion and drumset parts), and most of the rhythms are notated as repeated two-bar patterns. This book also includes a tuning and maintenance section packed with tips to help keep your equipment in good condition. A glossary of terms is located at the end of the book.

NOTATION KEY

Drumset

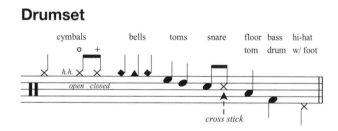

Percussion

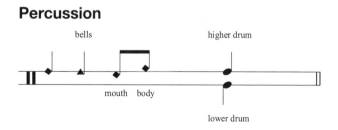

Congas–Bongós–Drums

RHYTHM & PERCUSSION

BLUES

Blues is one of the most celebrated forms of American music and comes from the mixture of Negro spiritu-als, dance music and chants. It started as a type of *a cappella* folk song, and has since evolved into different forms of instrumentation. The standard blues form is known as a "12-bar blues," and the triplet-based *shuffle* can be notated in simple meter with triplets ($\frac{4}{4}$) or in compound meter ($\frac{12}{8}$).

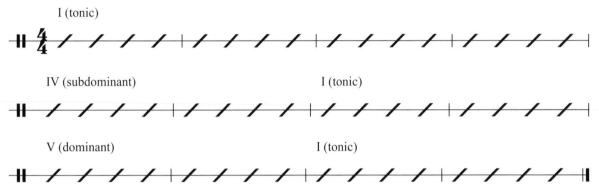

BLUES · Standard Shuffle

Slow Blues in ⁴⁄₄

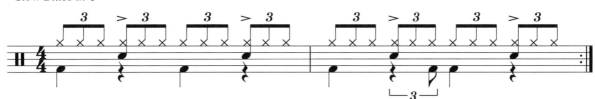

Variation

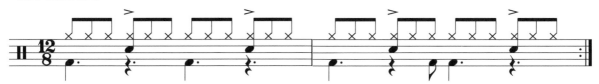

Slow Blues in ¹²⁄₈

Variation

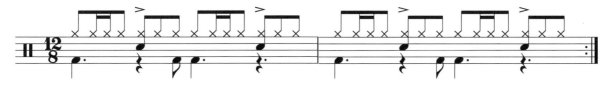

BLUES · Chicago Shuffle

Chicago Shuffle in 4/4

Variation

Chicago Shuffle in 12/8

Variation

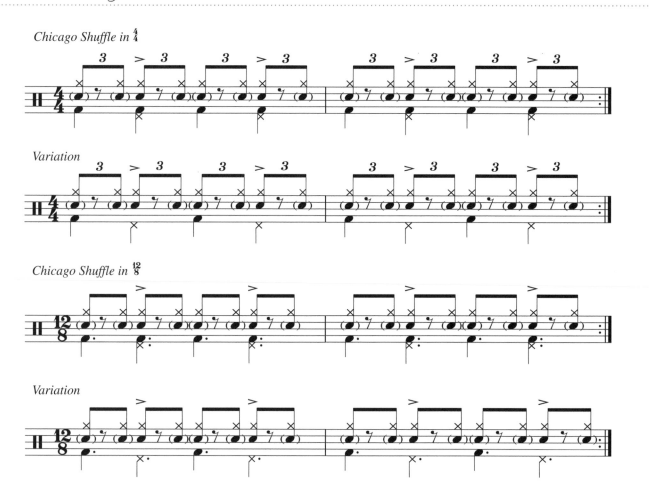

BLUES · Upbeat Shuffle

Upbeat Shuffle in 4/4

Variation

Upbeat Shuffle in 12/8

Variation

Ghost-Note Shuffle in 4/4

Variation

Ghost-Note Shuffle in 12/8

Variation

CAJUN

Cajun is a folk rhythm that emerged from the French-Canadian influence during the eighteenth century in New Orleans, Louisiana. These rhythms are usually played on a drumset.

Drumset

Variation

Waltz in 3

Variation

Slow in 9

Variation

CALYPSO

Calypso is a French rhythm that originated in the Caribbean islands (most notably Trinidad) during the 1950s. Calypso was a folk-type song form originally played by large ensembles until the appearance of steel drums. Nowadays, the calypso rhythm can be heard both in steel drum ensembles and in other different small-group bands.

COUNTRY

This style of folk music originated in the United States through the influence of Irish and Scottish immigrants, and originally revolved around instruments like the fiddle and the banjo. Here are some of the most representative examples of country music:

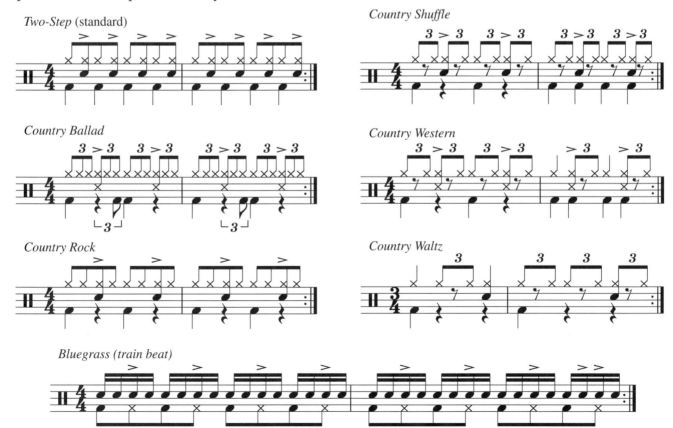

DISCO

Disco is a rhythm that developed in the mid-seventies. It has its roots in soul and funk music, with elements of rock.

DRUM & BASS

Drum & Bass is a style that is based on techno (electronic) music with elements of reggae and hip-hop. The basic principle is based on a repeating drum pattern with small variations added to create what is called a *loop*. The Drum & Bass sound is generally created by sequencers (drum machines), DJs, and programmers, but it is often backed up by a live drummer.

FUNK · Standard Funk

Funk is a style that has its roots in jazz, rock and soul music. It is a syncopated rhythm that became popular in the sixties and achieved its peak popularity in the mid-seventies.

FUNK · New Orleans Funk

This style is modeled after Creole marching bands and is widely played in brass ensembles as well as drum corps.

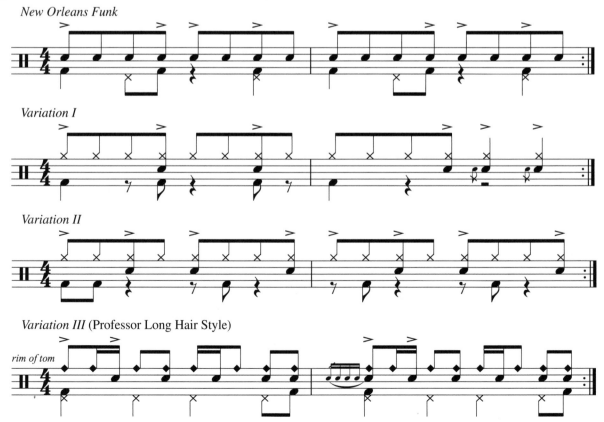

FUNK · Linear Funk

The peculiarity of this style lies in the fact that no limbs play at the same time. This style is usually played in sixteenth notes.

FUNK · Funk Rock

This style is less syncopated and has more of a straight feel. It incorporates elements of rock and pop.

GOSPEL

Gospel is an African-American rhythm that has its roots in the blues, and is widely played in African-American Baptist churches. The success of this genre is due in part to the early and consistent promotion of one of its most prominent enthusiasts, Thomas A. Dorsey.

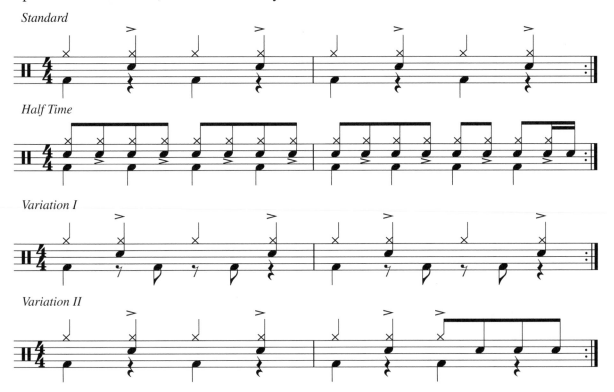

HEAVY METAL

Heavy metal is a fast-tempo music that has its origin in rock. Among its most characteristic features are distorted guitars, challenging rhythms, high-pitched or growling vocals, and double bass drum patterns.

HIP-HOP · Hip-Hop 1

Hip-hop is a concoction of styles ranging from Rhythm & Blues to rock and funk. With the increasing popularity of rap in the mid-eighties and the technological revolution of sequencers and drum machines, this style took on a major role on the mainstream music scene. Today, live musicians are becoming a standard element in this music, sometimes even with two drummers playing simultaneously.

HIP-HOP · Hip-Hop 2

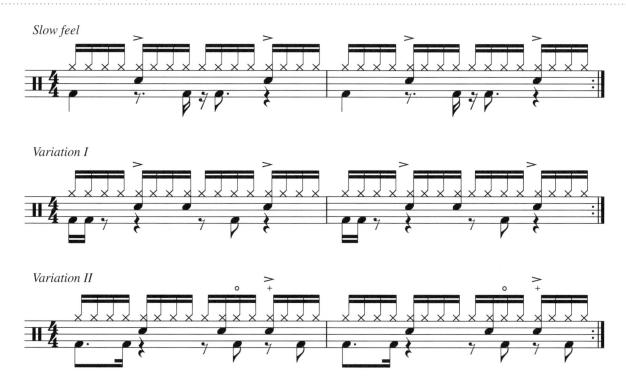

JAZZ

Jazz is the quintessential American music. With its roots in African-American music, jazz is the result of a multifaceted mix of different influences assimilated in New Orleans in the early 1900s, and is characterized by extensive use of the "swing" feel. Some of the main styles of jazz are Dixieland (1900–1920), big band (1920–1950), bebop (1940–1950), cool jazz (1950–1960), and avant-garde (1960s).

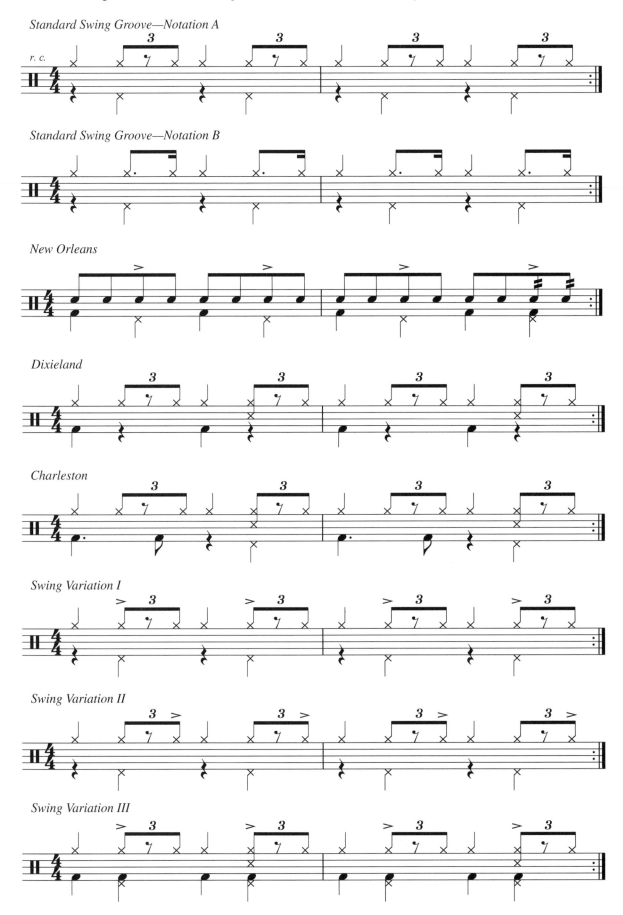

JAZZ

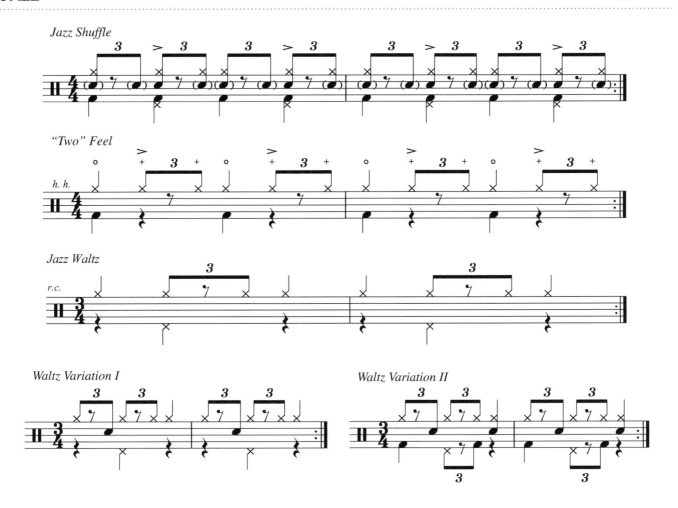

Jazz Shuffle

"Two" Feel

Jazz Waltz

Waltz Variation I

Waltz Variation II

KLEZMER

This style comes from the rich musical tradition of the Jewish population of Eastern Europe. The rhythms presented here are adaptations of the traditional rhythms for the drumset. Among the most popular rhythms of this style are the *bulgar*, the *freylakhs*, the *hora*, the *khosidl*, and the *terkisher*.

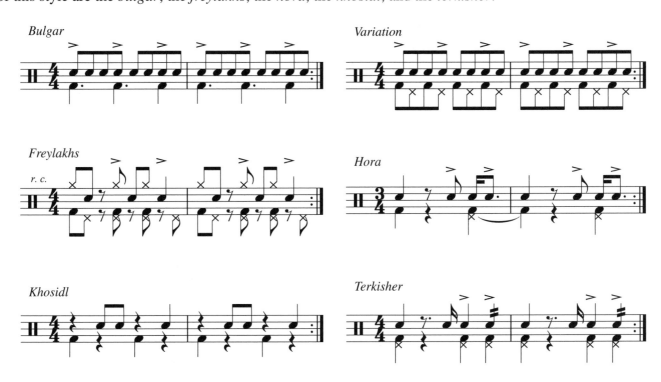

Bulgar

Variation

Freylakhs

Hora

Khosidl

Terkisher

MARCH

March is the traditional rhythm written for marching in two-step time. Originally, the march was used for military processions.

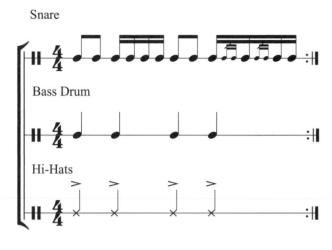

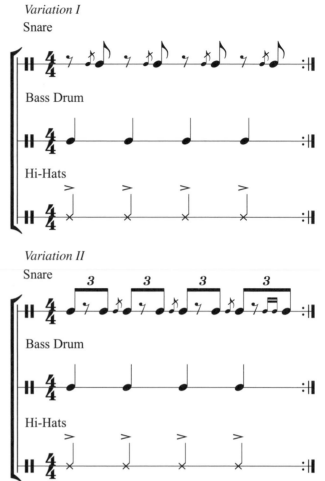

NEW ORLEANS (SECOND LINE)

The *Second Line* used to be (and to some degree still is) a brass and percussion marching band used in parades and/or funerals, depending on the occasion. This rhythm has been adapted to the drumset and is one of the cornerstones of swing.

REGGAE (ONE DROP)

Reggae is a Jamaican style that has elements of ska, Rhythm & Blues, and Afro-Jamaican rhythms. It started in the fifties following the popularity of calypso and ska, and became very popular during the sixties and seventies thanks to Bob Marley and the Wailers. The most characteristic feature of this rhythm is the synchronized hit of the bass and snare drum cross-stick (rim) on the third beat.

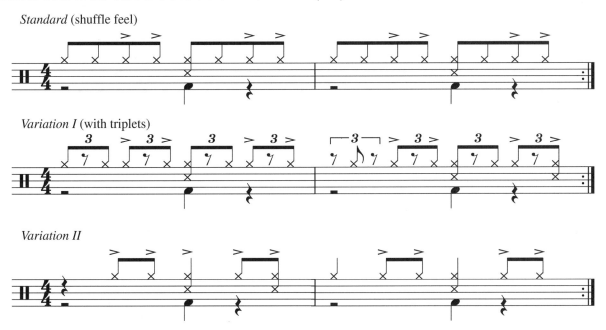

ROCK

The *rock* beat is the most popular and influential rhythm in pop music. Rock has been around since the fifties, and is a combination of jazz and Rhythm & Blues. The following examples are just some of the most common and popular rock rhythms.

ROCK

Surf

Train Beat

Half-Time Feel

Classic Two-Beat

Bass Drum Patterns

Variation I

Variation II

Variation III

Variation IV

ROCK

Snare Drum Patterns

Variation I

Variation II

Variation III

Variation IV

Alternative-Rock Patterns

Variation I

Variation II

Variation III

Variation IV

SKA

Ska is a Jamaican rhythm that started in the 1950s, and is a mixture of rock 'n' roll, jazz, and Rhythm &
Blues. Ska's feel is very similar to reggae since both rhythms emphasize the third beat of each measure.
Another characteristic of ska is the "four on the floor" pulse in the bass drum.

SOCA

Soca is a rhythm from the island of Trinidad that became popular in the 1970s. It is essentially a faster,
modern version of calypso.

WALTZ

This Austrian dance in $\frac{3}{4}$ is still very popular today. The *waltz* rhythm started in the late eighteenth century, and reached its height of popularity in the middle decades of the nineteenth century.

ZYDECO

Zydeco is a form of Louisiana Creole dance music closely related to Cajun, with Caribbean and African influences. Zydeco is played with a button accordion (or the less-traditional keyboard accordion) and a *frottoir* (a washboard or "rubboard" percussion instrument worn on the chest).

JAZZ, FUNK, & FUSION

EARLY JAZZ · Big Sid Catlett

"Big Sid" Catlett came to prominence in New York City in the early thirties playing with big bands, and continued to be one of the busiest drummers for small groups until the early fifties. Although he had a fine technique, Catlett chose to play behind Benny Goodman, Teddy Wilson, Louis Armstrong, and all the other great soloists of his time in an effort to get the music to swing. He was musically flexible and played comfortably with early big bands such as McKinney's Cotton Pickers, pre-modern Louis Armstrong, and the bebop of Charlie Parker and Dizzy Gillespie. Fiery rimshots were one of his identifiable features, as was his style of playing time on the hi-hat with sticks instead of on the ride cymbal and snare with brushes. He has had an enormous influence on the drummers who have followed him.

EARLY JAZZ · Chick Webb

Chick Webb was perhaps the most revered and influential drummer of the early big band era. He was a major influence on Buddy Rich and Louie Bellson, among others. Although he swung hard, Webb also showcased his technique and was one of the first to place the drummer in the spotlight as a featured soloist. Although he often played time on the hi-hat, he was one of the first to orchestrate band arrangements with rimshots and fills around the kit in soloist fashion.

EARLY JAZZ · George Wettling

Considered one of Dixieland's greatest drummers, Wettling was one of the first to shift the timekeeping from the bass drum to the hi-hat and ride cymbal. He also had an ability to change patterns and colors behind each soloist, giving them their own spotlight and sound.

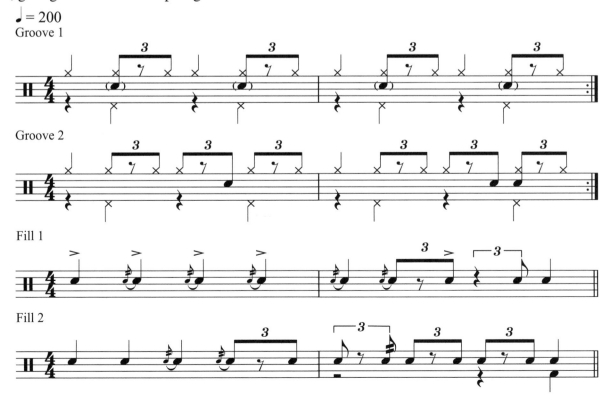

CLASSIC JAZZ · Papa Jo Jones

Jones was also one of the first to shift the timekeeping from the bass drum to the hi-hat and ride cymbal—particularly the hi-hat. He was the driving force behind the Count Basie Band. His focus on the hi-hat was a major influence on the drummers who followed him, and he would often take complete solos on the hi-hat alone.

CLASSIC JAZZ · Kenny Clarke

Kenny Clarke helped define bebop drumming and further developed the shift of timekeeping from the bass drum and hi-hat to the ride cymbal. Where his predecessors played steady patterns on the bass drum and snare while playing time on the ride cymbal, Clarke freed up the bass drum and snare with more complex accents and patterns. He would often play "bombs" behind soloists, earning him the nickname "Klook."

CLASSIC JAZZ · Gene Krupa

Known for his snare press rolls and showmanship, Krupa recorded the first extended drum solo on "Sing, Sing, Sing" with Benny Goodman. Along with Chick Webb, Krupa brought the drummer further out from the back line and into the limelight. He is generally recognized as the most famous drummer who ever lived.

CLASSIC JAZZ • Max Roach

Max Roach internalized the drumming vocabulary that came before him and took it to a level that changed the sound and shape of drumming forever. He was the first to break up the steady ride pattern into countless variations and he developed the freedom of the snare and bass drum, being perhaps the first to recognize the hi-hat as an ornamentation of time rather than playing it consistently on two and four. Roach also further developed the drums as a melodic solo instrument and introduced possibilities that set a new standard in drumming. He achieved this over several decades—first as a sideman with Charlie Parker, Miles Davis, and Dizzy Gillespie, then as a band leader.

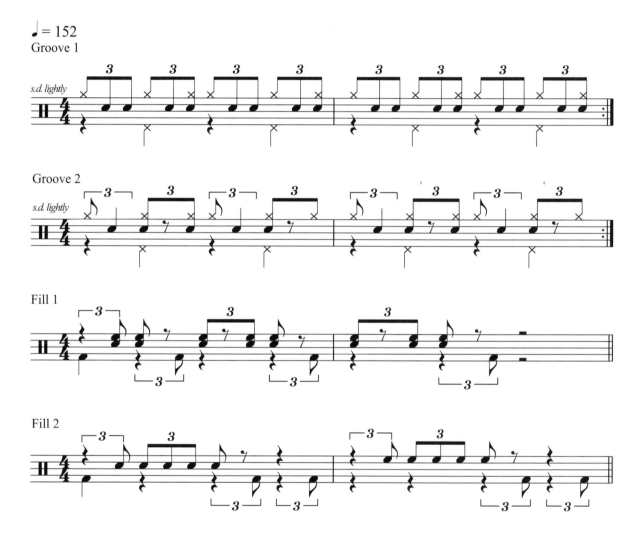

CLASSIC JAZZ · Buddy Rich

Although Rich appears on quintessential recordings with Charlie Parker and Dizzy Gillespie, it is for his influence as a big band drummer/leader that he's widely known. Aside from Gene Krupa, Rich is considered the most famous drummer. He further developed the groundwork laid down by Chick Webb and Gene Krupa as a showman and technician. He found new ways to orchestrate band arrangements around the drum kit with speed and four-way coordination.

CLASSIC JAZZ • Jimmy Cobb

Cobb's greatest contribution is the deep groove and swing that he laid down behind many of the greatest jazz musicians. Rather than showcase the drummer as a soloist, his main focus was paving the way with the ride cymbal as the main groove, ornamented with tasteful bass drum and snare accents, resulting in a rich, warm sound from the kit.

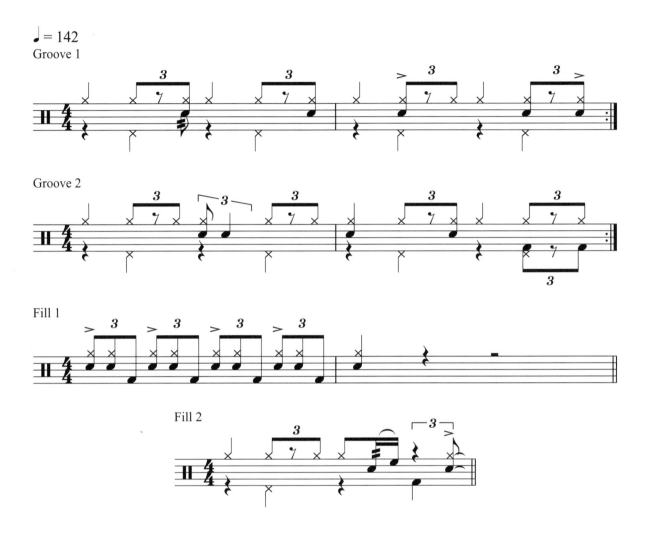

CLASSIC JAZZ · Ed Thigpen

Thigpen set the standard for jazz piano/bass/drums trio playing with Oscar Peterson and Ray Brown. His focus is keeping a swinging, steady groove. Due to the acoustic nature of this ensemble, Thigpen often leaned toward using brushes and consequently developed new vocabulary and techniques in that area.

MODERN JAZZ · Joe Morello

Morello's most famous recording is "Take Five" with Dave Brubeck, where he takes one of the most recognized and featured drum solos in recorded history and put the drums further in the limelight. His use of space and sense of color and orchestration around the kit is a tasteful contribution to jazz drumming.

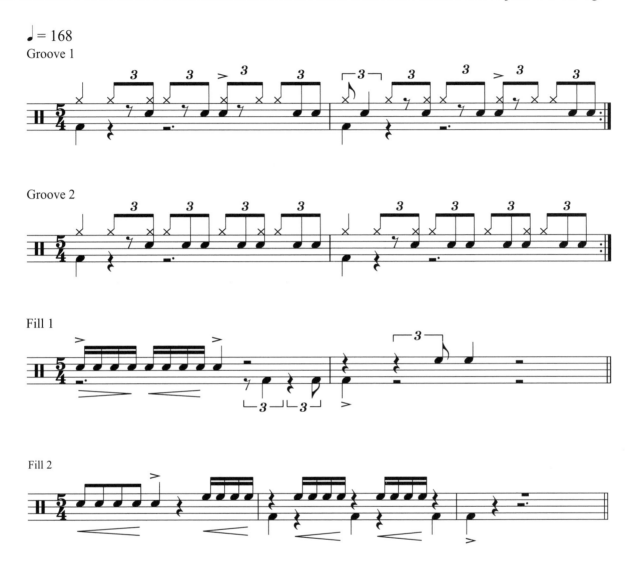

MODERN JAZZ · Elvin Jones

Elvin Jones had perhaps the most individual approach to jazz drumming of all. His use of triplets with his left hand is unique from any other drummer that came before him. The "wall of sound" he created in his drum solos is difficult to decipher because of the personal way it is executed. One of the most identifiable aspects of his playing is the powerful, swinging groove he always created.

♩ = 160
Groove 1

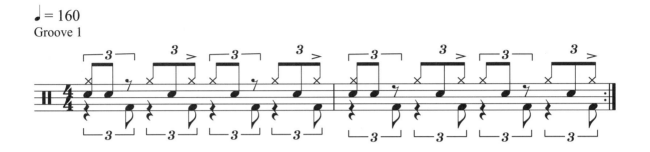

Groove 2

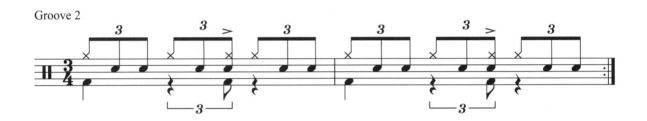

Fill 1

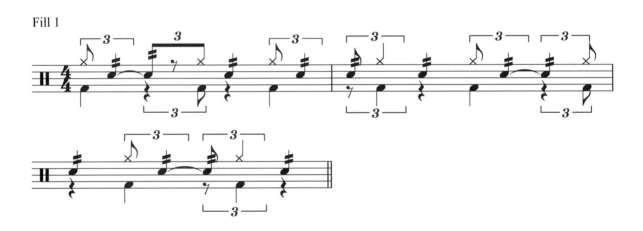

Fill 2

MODERN JAZZ · Roy Haynes

Roy Haynes's career spans six decades beginning with Charlie Parker and Miles Davis, then John Coltrane, Chick Corea, Pat Metheny, and, eventually, his own bands. Having roots in bebop, Haynes expanded that knowledge to modern drumming by finding new ways to accentuate time playing. He paved the way by changing the shape and patterns of ride cymbal timekeeping, augmenting it with more complex and independent accents with the bass drum and snare, and including the hi-hat as ornamentation rather than keeping time with it on two and four.

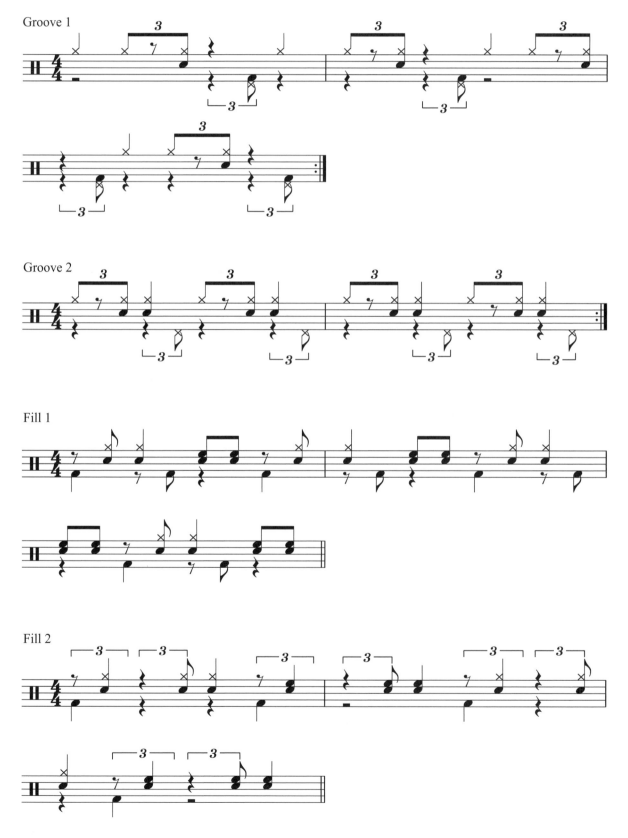

MODERN JAZZ · Tony Williams

Tony Williams changed the sound and approach of jazz drumming perhaps more than any other. He combined all the bebop elements that came before him with the more recent experimentations of Roy Haynes and others, and molded it all into adventurous, fiery and groundbreaking performances with the Miles Davis Quintet. Williams went on to further experiment with elements of rock and again changed the sound and approach of jazz drumming, being perhaps the first true fusion drummer. His use of polyrhythms, four-way coordination, playing the hi-hat on all quarter notes instead of two and four, and his development of playing hi-hat accents, has had—along with Elvin Jones—a major impact on modern jazz and fusion drumming.

MODERN JAZZ · Jack DeJohnette

Coming into prominence slightly after contemporary Tony Williams, DeJohnette, like Elvin Jones, has one of the most unique and individual approaches to drumming. His melding of bebop, Tony Williams, and Elvin Jones into his own personal sound has graced performances with Miles Davis, Jaco Pastorius, Betty Carter, and numerous others. Like Elvin Jones, his "wall of sound" fills and solos are difficult to decipher because of their personal nature.

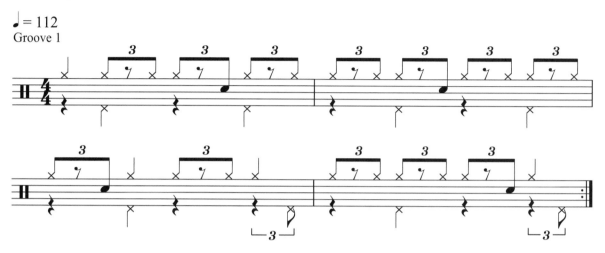

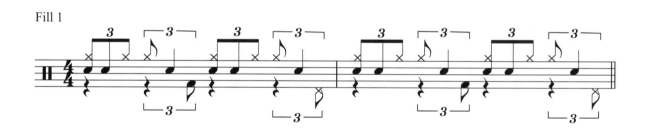

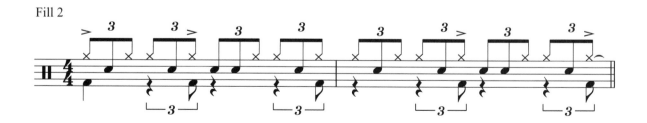

FUNK AND RHYTHM & BLUES · Al Jackson

Al Jackson is the driving force behind much of sixties and seventies soul music, having played with Booker T. & the MG's and on many of the Hi and Stax Records sessions. His style is deceptively simple, but his force and emphasis on the groove has not often been matched.

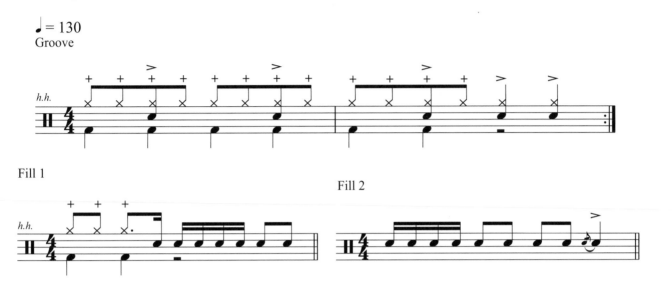

FUNK AND RHYTHM & BLUES · John "Jabo" Starks

The drummer behind most of James Brown's recordings and live performances, Starks brought his background as a jazz drummer to funk. He interpreted the even-eighth quality of funk playing with a slight swing-triplet edge, placing the groove somewhere between even and swing. Changing the backbeat from the steady two and four to unorthodox, staggered placements was a major innovation of Starks's.

FUNK AND RHYTHM & BLUES · Clyde Stubblefield

Stubblefield joined John "Jabo" Starks in James Brown's band, and together they created the quintessential bible of funk drumming.

FUNK AND RHYTHM & BLUES · Bernard Purdie

Purdie is known for his great groove and funk backbeat. The drummer on countless hits and historic recordings for Aretha Franklin, among others, he tunes his snare tight and favors his rimshot backbeat over the silky time of his right hand—either on the hi-hat or ride. He created some signature grooves that lent themselves perfectly to the songs he was recording.

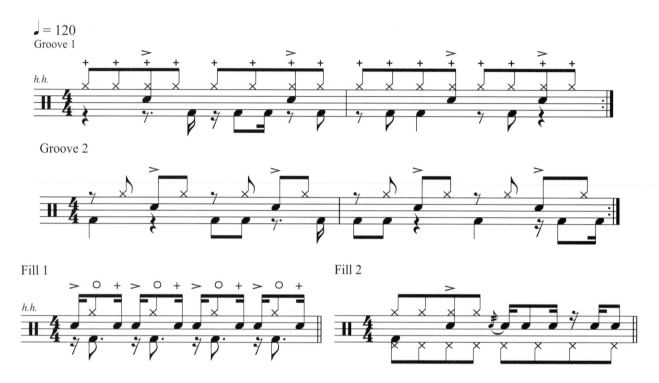

FUNK AND RHYTHM & BLUES · Harvey Mason

Best known for his unique funk groove on Herbie Hancock's "Chameleon," Mason has recorded and performed with a "Who's Who" list of artists. Along with Tony Williams, he is one of the first to fuse swing with even-eighth feels, but in a funky Purdie/Stubblefield/Starks direction.

FUNK AND RHYTHM & BLUES · David Garibaldi

Garibaldi is known as one of the innovators of funk drumming through his work with Tower of Power. Like the modern jazz drummers that freed up the snare, hi-hat, and bass drum, instead of keeping straight time, Garibaldi created endless variations of snare drum, hi-hat, and bass drum placements and combinations with incredible independence, while maintaining a deep, funky groove.

FUNK AND RHYTHM & BLUES · Mike Clark

Mike Clark, along with David Garibaldi, paved the way in funk music by experimenting with different combinations of hi-hat, bass drum, and snare placements in a funky setting. As the drummer after Harvey Mason in Herbie Hancock's Headhunters band, Clark incorporated the use of polyrhythms introduced by Tony Williams, becoming not only a funk innovator, but also an early proponent of fusion music.

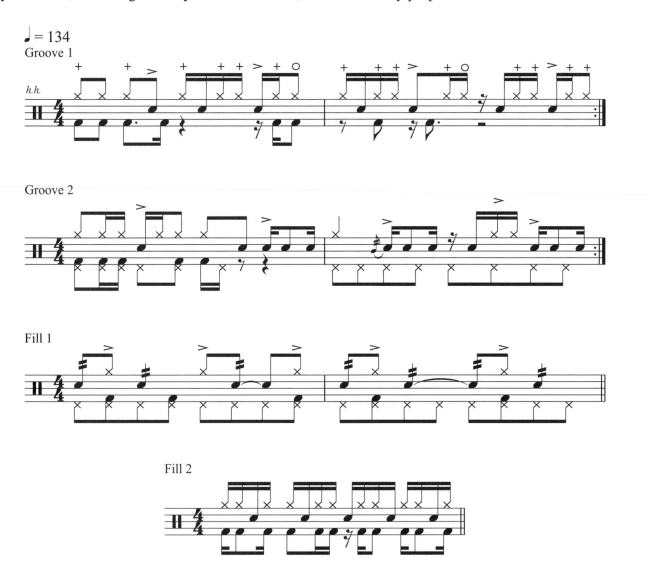

FUSION · Airto Moreira

Moreira introduced a Brazilian percussionist's approach to drumming. As the percussionist in the original Weather Report band, Airto went on to play drum kit in Chick Corea's Light as a Feather band, then recorded several solo albums. His technique is somewhat unorthodox, and although he's an incredible time-keeper, his interpretation of fills and drum orchestration is undoubtedly derived from a percussionist's point of view. He is an early fusion pioneer with a different angle.

FUSION · Billy Cobham

Cobham, like Tony Williams, greatly changed the approach to drums while he was a member of John McLaughlin's Mahavishnu Orchestra. He combined in an innovative way the use of the double bass drum setup of earlier drummers such as Cozy Cole, Louie Bellson and Ed Shaughnessy, and the polyrhythms of Tony Williams, in addition to rock, jazz and funk influences. The speed and power of his single-stroke roll orchestrated over his multiple-tom setup is unparalleled.

FUSION · Terry Silverlight

Silverlight is one of fusion's early pioneers, having played on the 1971 Barry Miles album *White Heat* along with Pat Martino, Lew Tabackin and John Abercrombie. The album is considered a turning point in the progress of jazz and inspired many of today's foremost fusion artists, including Pat Metheny. Silverlight's melding of various influences in that period, such as Tony Williams, Max Roach, British pop music and classical music, naturally led him to become a successful studio musician playing on hit records in a variety of styles.

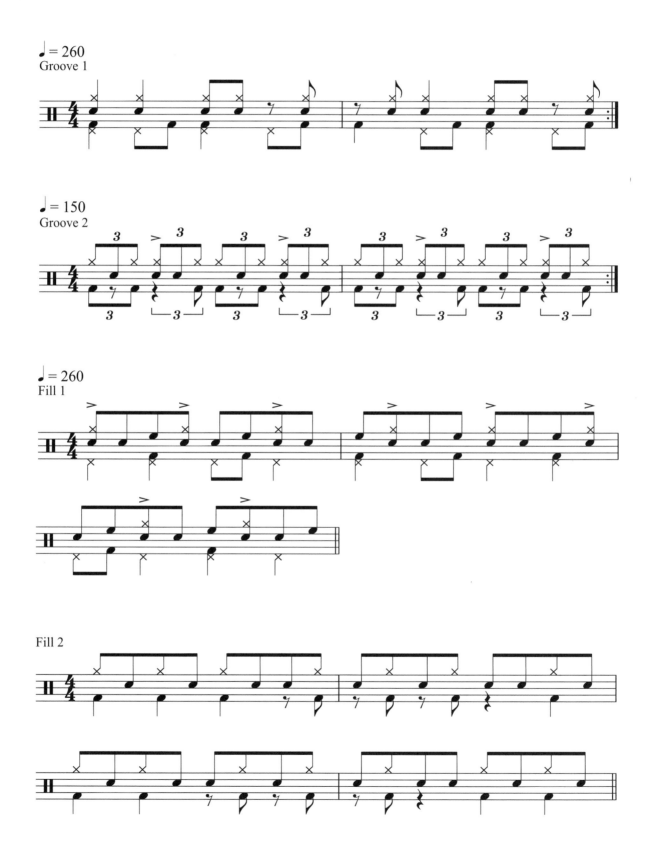

FUSION • Steve Gadd

Gadd was the first drummer since Tony Williams to impact drumming on an exceptionally high level, and remains unmatched to this day. He has an uncanny ability to mold his playing to any musical style and contribute the most complimentary drumming possible for each project, all while maintaining his own original sound. The grooves he's created are classic, and the virtuosic patterns and fills he's developed in the jazz, fusion and pop categories have influenced almost every drummer since.

♩ = 88
Groove 1

♩ = 120
Groove 2

♩ = 88
Fill 1

♩ = 120
Fill 2

FUSION · Rick Marotta

One of the busiest pop/funk drummers of the seventies, Marotta played the classic funk groove on Steely Dan's "Peg" and many other hit recordings. Although his influences are Steve Gadd, Harvie Mason and other funk greats, his approach is simple, and the focus is on the importance and depth of a good groove, always contributing to an original performance.

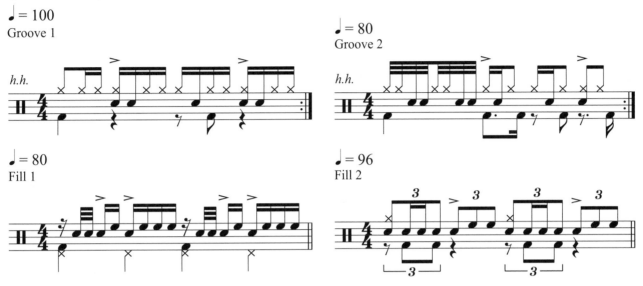

FUSION · Steve Jordan

A contemporary of Steve Gadd, Rick Marotta, and other studio session players of the seventies, Jordan's focus is on the funkiness and power of the groove. He possesses exceptional originality and commands an enviable technique, yet his ear for the groove has successfully linked his countless jazz, fusion, rock and funk recordings.

FUSION · Peter Erskine

Erskine has successfully packaged the influences of Steve Gadd, Jack DeJohnette and other drummers before him, by way of technical accuracy and execution. He has helped set the standard for current-day jazz/fusion drummers.

FUSION · Horacio Hernández

Hernández has brought to contemporary jazz/fusion drumming an element similar to what Airto Moreira brought three decades earlier. He has incorporated his Latin and percussion influences, thus creating a new approach to the drum kit. His ability to play the clave pattern with his left foot and coordinate intricate rhythms around the kit with precision is groundbreaking.

FUSION · Vinnie Colaiuta

Along with Peter Erskine, Colaiuta has set the standard for the contemporary jazz/fusion drummer. He has taken the best of the jazz/fusion pioneers and combined it into a pristine presentation. His diversity has placed him on countless recordings in the pop and rock fields as well.

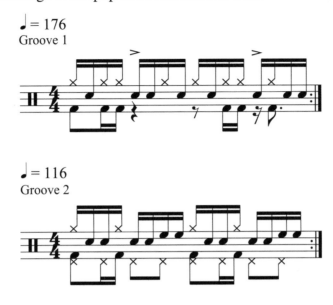

BRUSH PATTERNS

Many patterns have been developed for brushes. Here are five examples, to be played on the snare drum. Each of these patterns is in $\frac{4}{4}$ time, but they can be adjusted for other time signatures. Tempo is about 50 bpm except where indicated otherwise.

Soup

Place both brushes at twelve o'clock at the top of the head. Pressing both brushes into the drum head, start on beat 1 and circle the perimeter of the drum with the left brush counter-clockwise and the right brush clockwise, finishing with both brushes at twelve o'clock on beat 2. Repeat this for each quarter note.

Soup-Tap

Place both brushes at twelve o'clock at the top of the head. Pressing both brushes into the drumhead, start on beat 1 and circle half the diameter of the drum with the left brush counter-clockwise and the right brush clockwise, ending by tapping both brushes at six o'clock on beat 2. Repeat this for beats 3 and 4.

Half Moon

Beginning on beat 1, place the left brush at nine o'clock and the right brush at three o'clock. Drag the left brush clockwise ending on beat 2 at twelve o'clock and the right brush counter-clockwise ending on beat 2 at twelve o'clock. Repeat this motion for beats 3 and 4. As a variation, add taps with the right brush on the "and" of 2 and the "and" of 4 with a swing feel.

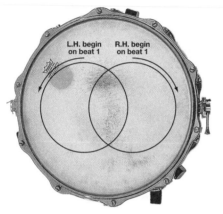

Complete each circle within a quarter note

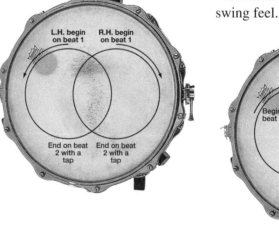

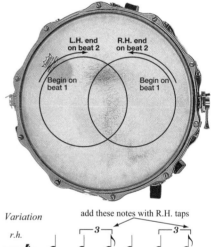

Circle and Tap

The left brush makes a smaller clockwise circle toward the center of the head starting at twelve o'clock on beat 1, completing the circle at twelve o'clock on beat 2. Repeat this for each quarter note. The right brush taps quarter notes toward the top of the head. As a variation, add taps with the right hand on the "and" of 2 and the "and" of 4 with a swing feel.

Samba Brush Groove

At the center of the head, swipe the left brush back and forth, with the downbeat quarter notes to the right and the upbeat eighth notes to the left. Accent beats 2 and 4. With the right hand toward the top of the head, tap a Latin bell pattern. Tempo can be 180 bpm or faster.

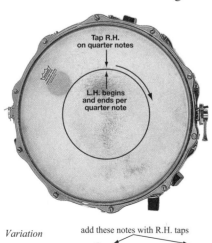

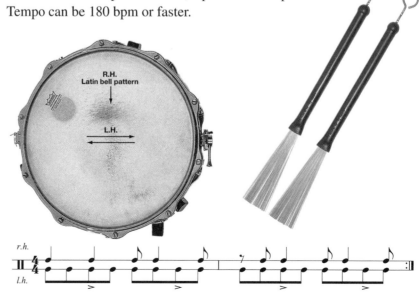

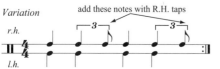

Single Strokes
Single-Stroke Roll

Single-Stroke Four

Single-Stroke Seven

Rolls
Multiple-Bounce Roll

Triple-Stroke Roll

Double-Stroke Roll

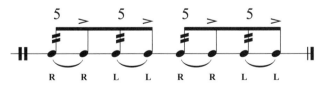

Five-Stroke Roll

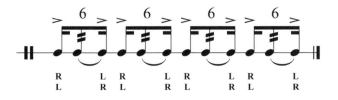

Six-Stroke Roll

Seven-Stroke Roll

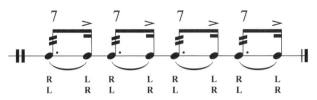

Nine-Stroke Roll

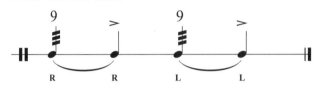

Ten-Stroke Roll

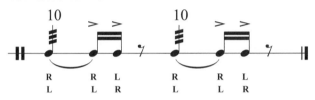

Eleven-Stroke Roll

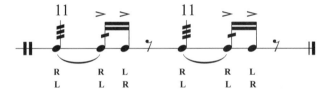

Thirteen-Stroke Roll

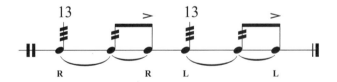

Fifteen-Stroke Roll

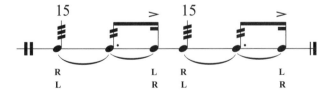

Seventeen-Stroke Roll

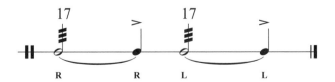

Flams

Flam

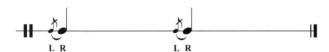

Flam Accent

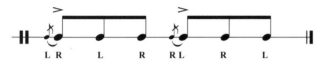

Flam Tap

Flamacue

Flam Paradiddle

Single-Flammed Mill

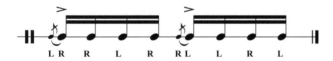

Flam Paradiddle-diddle

Pataflafla

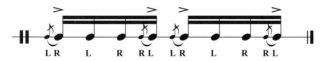

Swiss Army Triplet

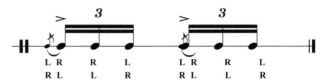

Inverted Flam Tap

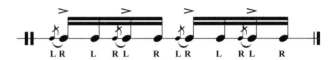

Flam Drag

Paradiddles

Single Paradiddle

Double Paradiddle

Triple Paradiddle

Paradiddle-diddle

RUDIMENTS · Drags / Ratamacues

Drags
Ruff

Single-Drag Tap

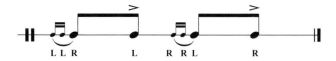

Double-Drag Tap

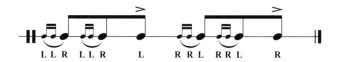

Single Dragadiddle

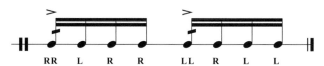

Drag Paradiddle #1

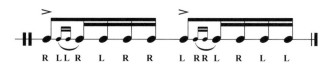

Drag Paradiddle #2

Ratamacues
Single Ratamacue

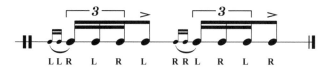

Double Ratamacue

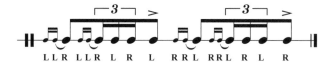

Triple Ratamacue

SELECTED DISCOGRAPHY

Big Sid Catlett

Armstrong, Louis. *The Complete RCA Victor Recordings* (RCA 63846)

—. *Louis Armstrong and His Orchestra, 1940-1942* (Classics 685)

Mike Clark

Hancock, Herbie. *Flood* (Sony 35439)

—. *Man-Child* (Sony International 9501)

—. *Thrust* (Sony International 86568)

The Headhunters. *Return of the Headhunters* (Verve Forecast 539028)

—. *Survival of the Fittest* (BMG International 140952)

Kenny Clarke

Clarke, Kenny. *Bohemia after Dark* (Savoy 107)

—. *Jazz Is Universal* (Atlantic 1401)

—. *Kenny Clarke in Paris, Vol. 1* (Disques Swing SW-8411)

—. *Klook's Clique* (Savoy 12083)

—. *The Quintessence* (Frémieax & Associés 235)

Jimmy Cobb

Cobb, Jimmy. *Cobb's Groove* (Milestone 9334)

Davis, Miles. *Kind of Blue* (Sony 1206)

Dorham, Kenny, and Cannonball Adderley. *Blue Spring* (Riverside/OJC 134)

Montgomery, Wes. *Full House* (Riverside/OJC OJCCD-106-2)

Billy Cobham

Benson, George. *White Rabbit* (Sony 64768)

Clarke, Stanely. *School Days* (Columbia 36975) Cobham, Billy. Crosswinds (Wounded Bird 7300)

—. *Spectrum* (Atlantic 7268)

—. *Total Eclipse* (Wounded Bird 8121)

Hubbard, Freddie. *Sky Dive* (Columbia ZK-44171)

Mahavishnu Orchestra with John McLaughlin. *Birds of Fire* (Sony 66081)

—. *Inner Mounting Flame* (Sony 65523)

Sebesky, Don. *Giant Box* (Sony 40697)

Vinnie Colaiuta

Bona, Richard. *Tiki* (Decca 0007178)

Corea, Chick. *The Ultimate Adventure* (Stretch 9045)

Dion, Celine. *Let's Talk About Love* (550 Music 68861)

Sting. *Ten Summoner's Tales* (A&M 540070)

Jack DeJohnette

Brecker, Michael. *Tales from the Hudson* (Impulse! 191)

Corea, Chick. *Sundance* (Charly 150)

Davis, Miles. *Live-Evil* (Columbia/Legacy 65135)

DeJohnette, Jack. *Extra Special Edition* (Capitol 30494)

Kloss, Eric. *Consciousness!* (Prestige 7793)

Pastorius, Jaco. *Word of Mouth* (Warner Bros. 2-3535)

Peter Erskine

Elias, Eliane. *Brazilian Classics* (Blue Note 84337)

Steps Ahead. *Modern Times* (Elektra 60351-2)

Weather Report. *8:30* (Columbia 57665)

—. *Night Passage* (Columbia CK-36793)

Steve Gadd

Clarke, Stanley. *Journey to Love* (Epic EK-36974)

Corea, Chick. *The Leprechaun* (Polygram 519798)

DiMeola, Al. *Land of the Midnight Sun* (Columbia CK-34074)

Mangione, Chuck. *Together* (Mercury SRM 2 7501)

Simon, Paul. *Still Crazy after All These Years* (Warner Bros. 2-25591)

Steely Dan. *Aja* (Universal/MCA 10077)

Streisand, Barbara. *Guilty* (Sony 36750)

Dave Garibaldi

Tower of Power. *Back to Oakland* (Warner Bros. 2-2749)

—. *Bump City* (Warner Bros. 2616)

—. *East Bay Grease* (Rhino R2-71145)

—. *Urban Renewal* (Warner Bros. 2834)

Roy Haynes

Corea, Chick. *Now He Sings, Now He Sobs* (Blue Note 38265)

Horacio "El Negro" Hernandez

Camilo, Michel. *Live at the Blue Note* (Telarc 83574)

—. *Thru My Eyes* (RMM 82067)

Hernandez, Horacio, and Robby Ameen. *Robby and Negro at the Third World War* (American Clave 1031)

Sanchez, David. *Street Scenes* (Columbia 67627)

Santana, Carlos. *Supernatural* (Arista 19080)

Al Jackson

Booker T. & the MG's. *Time Is Tight* (Stax 4424)

Franklin, Aretha. *30 Greatest Hits* (Atlantic 81668-2)

Green, Al. *Al Green's Greatest Hits* (DCC 1125)

Jackson, Al. *Atlantic Rhythm & Blues 1947-1974* [Box set] (Atlantic 82305-2)

Elvin Jones

Coltrane, John. *Live at Birdland* (Impulse! 198)

—. *Live at the Village Vanguard* (Impulse! 9005)

—. *A Love Supreme* (Impulse! 000061002)

—. *My Favorite Things* (Atlantic SD-1361-2)

Jones, Elvin. *Mr. Jones* (Blue Note BN A 110)

—. *On the Mountain* (Jazz Maniacs 5115)

Papa Jo Jones

Basie, Count. *Count Basie at Newport* (Verve 000161502)

—. *Count Basie: The Complete Decca Recordings* (GRD GRD-3-611)

Jones, Papa Jo. *The Essential Jo Jones* (Vanguard 101/2)

—. *The Main Man* (Pablo/OJC 869)

—. *Our Man Papa Jo!* (Denon 81757-7047-2)

—. *Smiles* (Black & Blue 975)

Steve Jordan

The Blues Brothers. *Made in America* (Atlantic 16025)

Fagen, Donald. *The Nightfly* (Warner Bros. 2-23696)

Spyro Gyra. *Carnaval* (MCA MCAD-1663)

Stern, Mike. *Upside Downside* (Atlantic 81656-2)

Young, Neil. *Landing on Water* (Geffen 490799)

SELECTED DISCOGRAPHY

Gene Krupa

Goodman, Benny. *Benny Goodman 1931-1933* (Classics 719)

—. *Benny Goodman and The Giants of Swing* (Decca GRD-609)

—. *Stompin' at the Savoy* (Bluebird/RCA 61067-2)

Hawkins, Coleman. *Coleman Hawkins 1929-1934* (Classics 587)

Waller, Fats. *Fats Waller and His Buddies* (Bluebird/RCA 61005-2)

Rick Marotta

Browne, Jackson. *The Very Best of Jackson Browne* (Rhino/Elektra 78091)

Garfunkel, Art. *Scissors Cut* (Columbia CK-37392)

Midler, Bette. *Bette Midler* (Atlantic 82779)

Roxy Music. *Avalon* (EMI 47438)

Scaggs, Boz. *Middle Man* (Columbia/Legacy 65626)

Simon, Paul. *There Goes Rhymin' Simon* (WEA/Rhino 12413)

Steely Dan. *Gaucho* (Universal 93129)

Taylor, James. *The Best of James Taylor* [2003] (Warner Bros. 73837)

Harvey Mason

Benson, George. *Breezin'* (Warner Bros. 2-3111)

Brecker Brothers. *Brecker Brothers Collection Vol. 1* (Novus 3075)

—. *Brecker Brothers Collection Vol. 2* (Novus 3076)

Hancock, Herbie. *Head Hunters* (Sony International 651239)

King, Carole. *Fantasy* (Columbia 34962)

Laws, Hubert. *Best of Hubert Laws* (Columbia ZK-45479)

Mason, Harvey. *Ratamacue* (Atlantic 82904)

—. *With All My Heart* (RCA Victor/BMG/Bluebird 52741)

Ritenour, Lee. *Captain Fingers* (Epic EK-34426)

Turrentine, Stanley. *Best of Mr. T* (Fantasy FCD-7708-2)

Washington, Jr., Grover. *Mister Magic* (Motown 5175)

Airto Moreira

Corea, Chick. *Return to Forever* (Universal 30313)

Mitchell, Joni. *Don Juan's Reckless Daughter* (Asylum 2-701)

Moreira, Airto. *Fingers* (CTI 6028)

—. *Seeds on the Ground* (Sequel NEX129)

—. *Struck by Lightning* (Caroline 1607)

Shorter, Wayne. *Native Dancer* (Columbia/Legacy CK-46159)

Joe Morello

Brubeck, Dave. *All the Things We Are* (Collectables 7724)

—. *Time Out* (Sony International 65122)

Morello, Joe. *Another Step Forward* (Ovation 1402)

—. *Going Places* (Digital Music Products [DMP] 497)

—. *It's About Time* (RCA PM-2486)

—. *The Joe Morello Sextet* (Intro 608)

Bernard Purdie

Curtis, King. *King Curtis: Live at Fillmore West* (Koch International 8024)

Franklin, Aretha. *Aretha Franklin: Live at Fillmore West* (WEA 71526)

—. *Young, Gifted and Black* (Rhino 71527)

King, B.B. *Guess Who* (Beat Goes On 71)

Buddy Rich

Rich, Buddy. *Big Swing Face* (Blue Note 37989)

—. *The Buddy Rich Big Band: New One!* (Pacific Jazz 94507B)

—. *Buddy Rich and His Orchestra: This One's for Basie* (Verve 817788-2)

—. *Buddy Rich in London* (RCA 4666)

—. *Buddy Rich Swinging* (Norgran MGN-26)

—. *Mr. Drums* (Quintessence Jazz 25051)

—. *The Roar of '74* (LRC Ltd. 24103)

Max Roach

Roach, Max. *At Basin Street* (EmArcy 534391)

—. *Deeds, Not Words* (Riverside/OJC OJCCD-304-2)

—. *Jazz at Massey Hall* (JVV Victor 41561)

—. *Percussion Bitter Sweet* (Impulse! 122)

Terry Silverlight

Benson, George. *Twice the Love* (Warner Bros. 2-25705)

Change. *Miracles* (East West 6111)

Grant, Tom. *In My Wildest Dreams* (Verve/Forecast 849530-2)

—. *Move Closer* (Jive/Novus 1214)

Manhattan Jazz Orchestra. *Bach 2000* (Milestone 9312)

—. *Hey Duke!* (Milestone 9320)

Miles, Barry. *Fusion Is…* (Century CRDD 1070)

—. *Zoot Suit Stomp* (Unidisc 2024)

Nyro, Laura. *Mother's Spiritual* (Line 900924)

Parris, Gil. *Blue Thumb* (Okra-tone 4969)

Silverlight, Terry. *Terry Silverlight* (Cymekab 809)

—. *Wild!* (Artist One-Stop 42)

Simon, John. *Out on the Street* (Vanguard 79470)

John "Jabo" Starks

Brown, James. *Dead on the Heavy Funk, 1975-1983* (Polydor 537901)

—. *Say It Loud—I'm Black and I'm Proud* (Polydor 841992)

—. *Star Time* (Polydor 849108)

Starks, John. *In the Jungle Groove* (Polydor 829624)

Clyde Stubblefield

B3 Bombers. *Live at the Green Mill CD* (Alltribe Records 724)

Brown, James. *20 All Time Greatest Hits* (Polydor 511326)

Ed Thigpen

Oscar Peterson Trio. *Night Train* (Verve 521440)

—. *We Get Requests* (Polygram 521442)

Thigpen, Ed. *Element of Swing* (Stunt 122)

—. *It's Entertainment* (Stunt 19816)

—. *Mr. Taste* (Justin Time 0043)

Chick Webb

Webb, Chick. *Featuring Ella Fitzgerald* (Empire 836)

—. *Rhythm Man* (Hep 1023)

—. *Standing Tall* (Drive Archive 42427)

—. *Stompin' at the Savoy: 1934/1939* (Epm Musique 159722)

—. *Strictly Jive* (Hep 1063)

SELECTED DISCOGRAPHY

George Wettling

Teagarden, Jack. *Father of Jazz Trombone* (Avid 126)

Waller, Fats. *The Very Best of Fats Waller* (Collectors' Choice
  Music 141)

Wettling, George. *Dixieland in Hi-Fi* (Harmony HL-7080)

—. *George Wettling's Jazz Band* (Columbia C 6189)

—. *George Wettling's Jazz Trios* (Kapp K-1028)

Tony Williams

Davis, Miles. *Four and More* (Sony 1212)

—. *Miles Smiles* (Sony 1216)

—. *My Funny Valentine* (Sony 1211)

—. *Nefertiti* (Sony 1218)

Williams, Tony. *Believe It* (Columbia PC 33836)

—. *Emergency!* (Polydor 849068)

—. *The Joy of Flying* (Sony 65473)

—. *Lifetime* (Blue Note 99004)

—. *Wilderness* (Ark 21 810053)

LATIN RHYTHM & PERCUSSION

$\frac{6}{8}$ (BEMBÉ)

This rhythm is believed to have originated from the Yoruba tribes of Nigeria, and was later brought to Cuba where it gained the popularity we know today. This rhythm can be played in both $\frac{6}{8}$ or in its increasingly popular $\frac{4}{4}$ form. The following rhythms are usually played on cowbells, *shekeres*, *congas* and/or adapted for drumset.

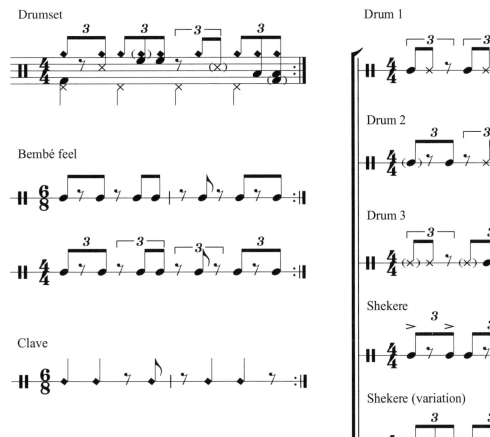

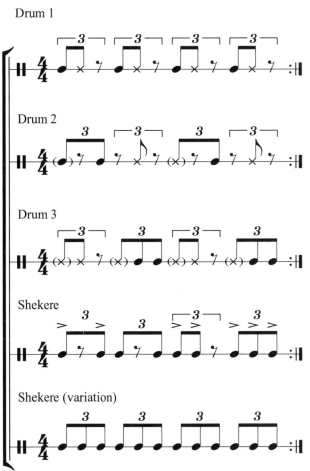

AFOXÉ

Afoxé is an Afro-Brazilian, semi-religious carnival procession from the state of Bahia. This music is the characteristic ritual music of *candomblé* (from the Yoruba tribe).

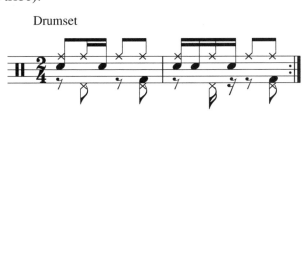

AFRICAN

This rhythm is sometimes called *abakwa*. It is usually played on different drums—especially on the side of the drums, in order to produce a wood-like sound. Abakwa originated as a rhythm played by a secret male slave society from western Africa.

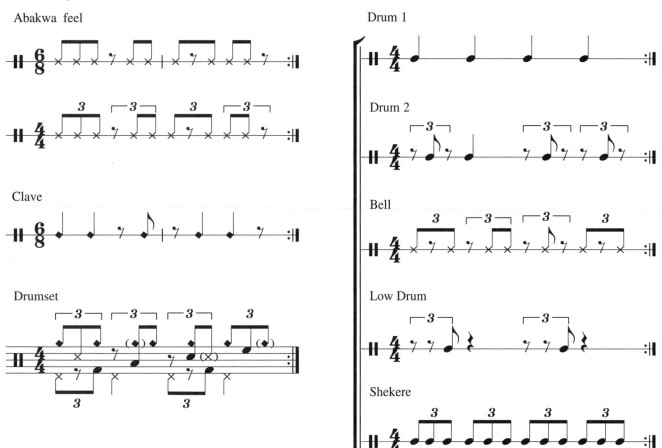

BAIAO

Baiao is a very popular Brazilian rhythm from the northeastern part of Brazil. The basic pattern is played on a *zabumba* (drum), a triangle and an accordion. Additional instruments include: *pandeiro* (tambourine), *ganzá* (shaker), *caxixis* (shakers), and *ago-gô* bells.

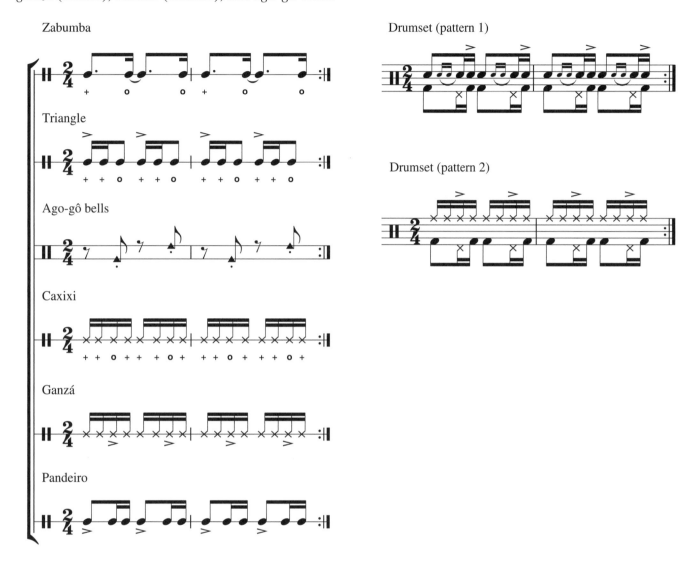

BATUCADA

Batucada, or *samba batucada*, is a type of samba played at the Rio de Janeiro carnival. This rhythm is played with percussion instruments only. Instruments include: *surdo* (low drum), *ganzá* (metal shaker), *caixa* (snare), *tamborim* (small tambourine), *ago-gô* bells, *cuica* (multi-timbral drum), *pandeiro* (tambourine), and *repinique* (double-headed drum).

BEGUINE

Beguine (also *biguine*) is a French Creole rhythm that originated during the nineteenth century on the islands of Guadeloupe and Martinique. It combines elements of polka with bélé (music from the islands of Saint Vincent and the Grenadines). Martinque musicians played three different styles of beguine: *beguine de salon*, *beguine de bal*, and *beguine de rue*. Beguine is one of the many musical styles that influenced the music of New Orleans.

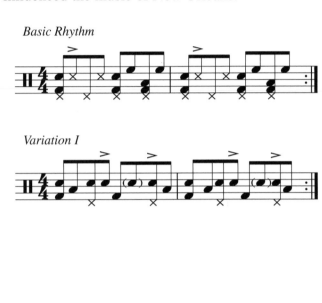

BOLERO

This rhythm was started in Cuba at the end of the nineteenth century. It is a kind of slow *son*, generally played in a ballad-style tempo, and is based on the Cuban *clave*. One of its more important ambassadors was Beny Moré.

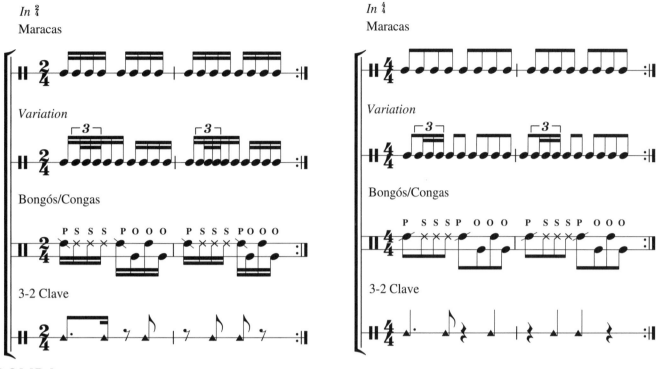

BOMBA

This is an Afro-Puerto Rican rhythm with a style similar to Afro-Cuban rhythms, more specifically, of the Bantu tribe. The playing of the clave is optional.

BONGO BELL

Bongo bell, or *campana* (Spanish for "bell"), is the typical rhythm played by the *bongosero* (bongo player) during certain sections of son, and helps to accentuate the downbeats.

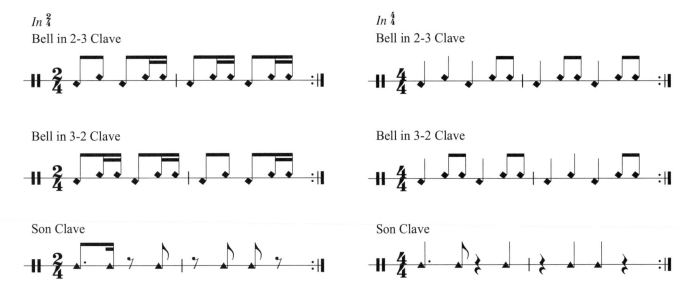

BOSSA NOVA

This rhythm is a combination of *samba de salão* (a $\frac{2}{4}$ rhythm with accents on beat 1) and *canção* (song), which is a Portuguese-based style. These, in addition to the influences of jazz and Cuban bolero, gave rise to *bossa nova*. Bossa nova is played by a small ensemble generally comprised of a singer accompanied by guitar, piano and drums.

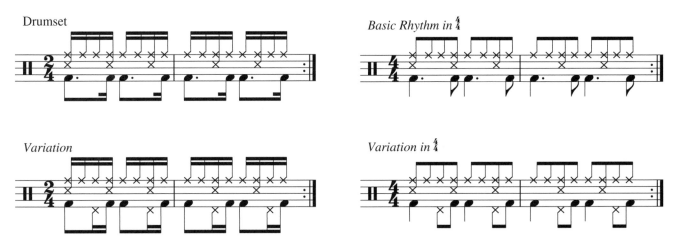

CÁSCARA

Cáscara ("shell" or "peel") is the name given to the specific pattern that is played on the side of the timbales or conga (shell). Cáscara is usually played during the verses in the *salsa* (modern son).

With 3-2 rumba clave

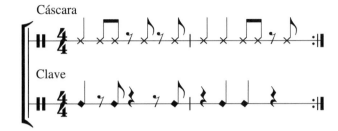

With 2-3 rumba clave

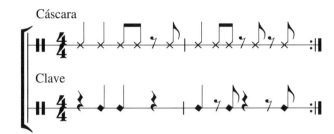

Variation with taps on timbal

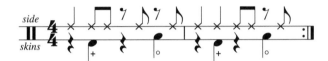

Variation with taps on timbal

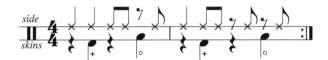

CATERETE

Caterete is a samba-based folk rhythm from Brazil.

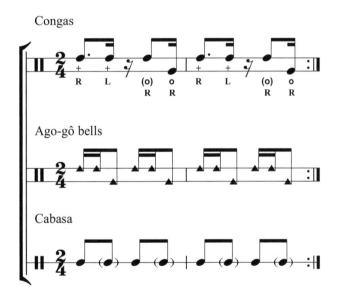

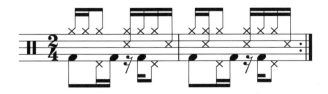

CHA-CHA-CHÁ

Cha-cha-chá was a popular dance in Cuba during the 1950s. Charanga orchestras comprised of piano, flute, violins, bass and timbales usually played this style.

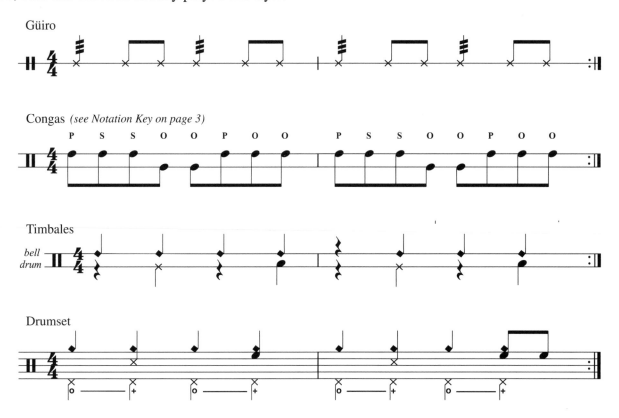

CHANGÜÍ

Changüí is one of the oldest Cuban genres. It originated in the early nineteenth century in the eastern region of the Guantánamo province. It combines elements of the Spanish *canción* with African rhythms and percussion instruments. The *tres* is essential to the changüí sound, which is thought to be the predecessor of modern son (or *son montuno*).

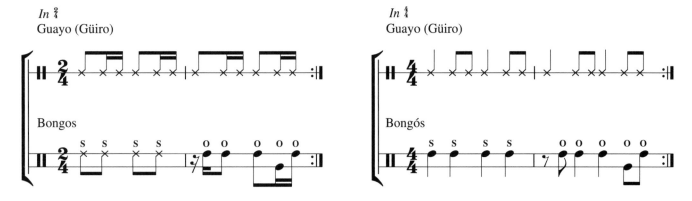

CLAVE

The term *clave* means "key," and for this reason is the most important rhythm in Afro-Cuban music. Whether **obvious** (sounding) or **implicit** (not sounding), the clave is always (as with most of these rhythms) present in the different Afro-Cuban rhythms and percussion patterns. The typical instrument used to play it is also called the *claves*, which is made of two pieces of wood that are struck to one another. The clave can be played on different instruments, such as on the side of timbales, congas, drumset, etc.

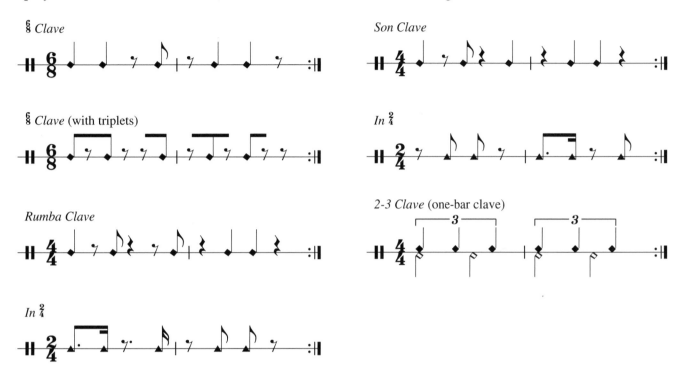

§ *Clave*

§ *Clave* (with triplets)

Rumba Clave

In 2/4

Son Clave

In 2/4

2-3 Clave (one-bar clave)

CONGA

Conga is a traditional Cuban rhythm that is played during the *comparsa* (or carnival) festival, usually played in large ensembles of percussionists, brass players, dancers and singers.

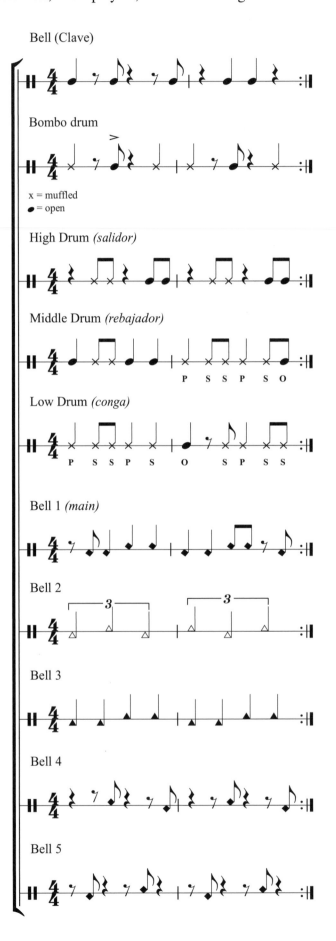

CUMBIA

Cumbia is one of the most popular Latin-American rhythms. The original folk cumbia originated on the North Atlantic coast of Colombia and was originally played with flutes, drums and accordion.

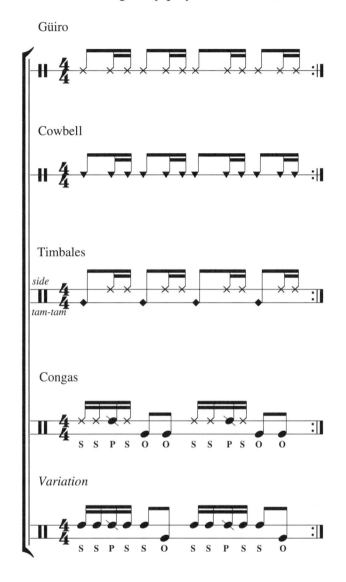

DANZÓN

Danzón is an Afro-Cuban rhythm with French influences (*contredanse*). This rhythm developed from a popular slow-dance form. In its more traditional form, danzón rhythm usually has a section played by violin and flute. The most important percussion instruments in the danzón are the claves and the timbal (timbale; **F** = finger tap).

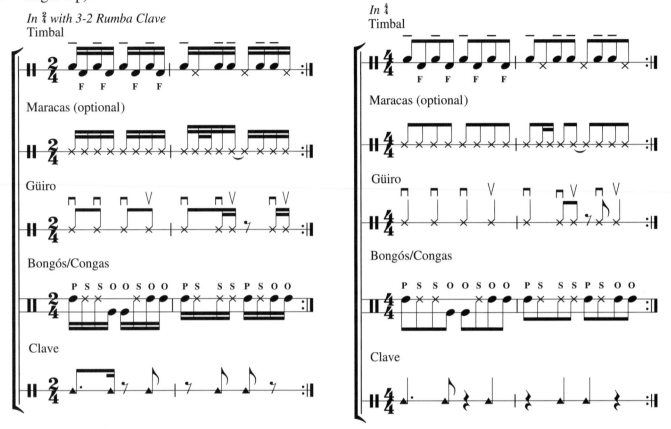

FORRÓ

Forró is a northeastern Brazilian rhythm. The traditional instrumentation for this style consists of accordion, zabumba and triangle. Forró is closely associated with samba, but is not quite the same. The emphasis of this rhythm falls on the first beat of every measure.

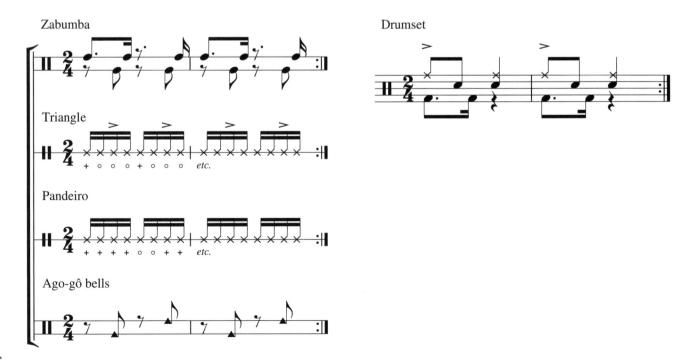

FREVO

Frevo is a kind of march from Recife, Pernambuco, in northeast Brazil. This rhythm is usually played with a fast and light feel.

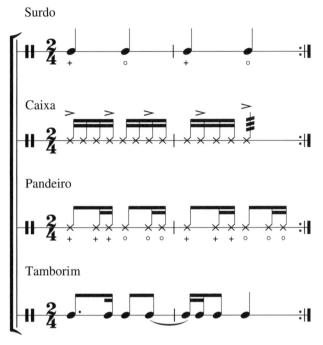

GUAGUANCÓ

This is the most popular form of the *rumba*, which is a folkloric Cuban rhythm. The drums used in the rhythm are: *quinto*, *salidor*, and *tres* (or *tres golpes*).

GUARACHA

Guaracha is one of the earliest forms of street music, and has satirical lyrics. A traditional Cuban peasant folk rhythm, the rhythmic structure of the guaracha resembles the traditional son style. The term guaracha is now widely used to mean a medium-tempo son.

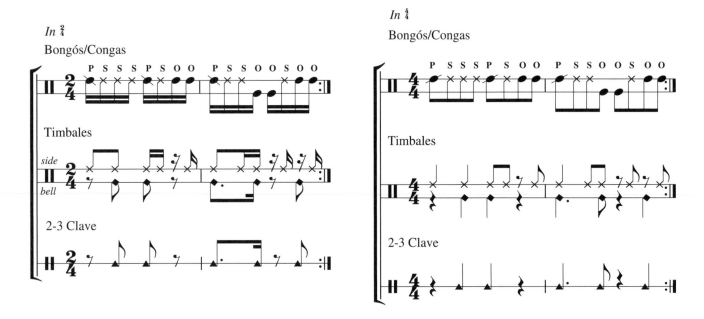

KIRIBÁ

Kiribá is one of the oldest and most traditional Cuban styles. It is a lyric and improvisational form typically played with tres, bongós, maracas, güiro and marímbula. Kiribá is widely played in Guantánamo province.

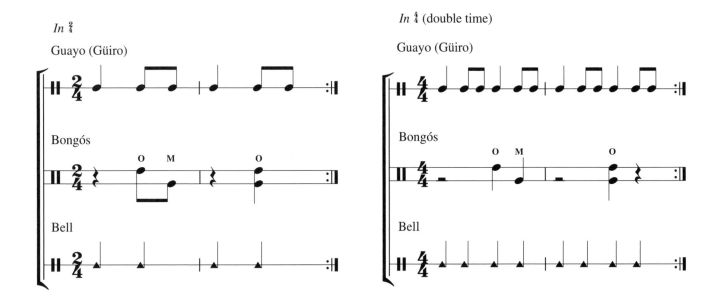

MAMBO

Mambo is an Afro-Cuban rhythm that was very popular in the 1940s and '50s. It is the result of one of the early fusions in modern Cuban instrumentation, since it is usually played with a large brass section (sometimes even with a big band). Pérez Prado was one of the main ambassadors of mambo music. He took his music first to Mexico and then to New York City, where it achieved worldwide recognition.

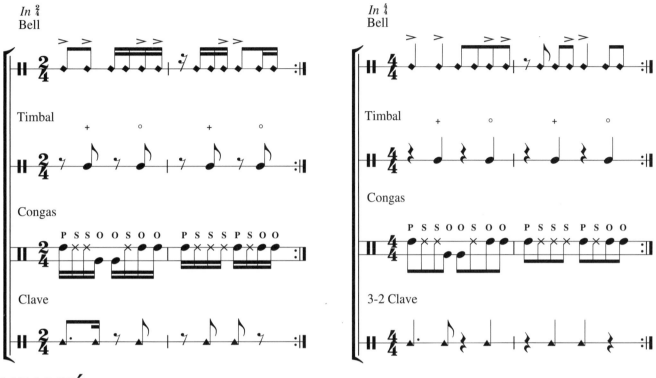

MARACATÚ

Maracatú was a procession rhythm used during the coronation ceremony for African kings. This rhythm is one of the most energetic, yet steady styles of Brazilian music. The use of a zabumba, a very large *bombo*—or bass drum—enhances the overall festive feeling.

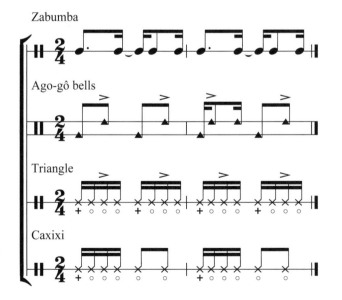

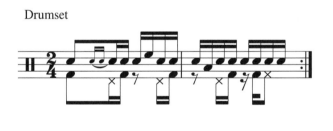

MERENGUE

Merengue is a folk dance and rhythm from the Dominican Republic with strong African and French roots. Merengue has three main parts: *merengue*, *jaleo* and *apanpichao*. Its typical instrumentation includes: tambora, güiro and accordion.

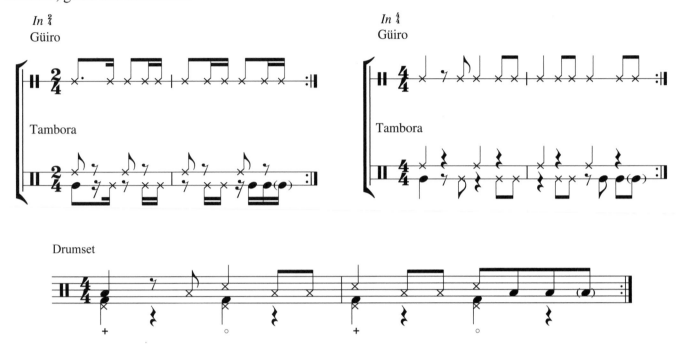

MOZAMBIQUE

Mozambique is a contemporary Afro-Cuban style created by Pedro Izquierdo (Pelo el Afrokan) around 1960. This rhythm combines traditional African and Afro-Cuban rhythms.

NANIGO

Nanigo is an Afro-Cuban secular dance loosely based on the forms and motifs of the abakwa rhythm. It is played with a large percussion ensemble, and is often played as a break section in son music.

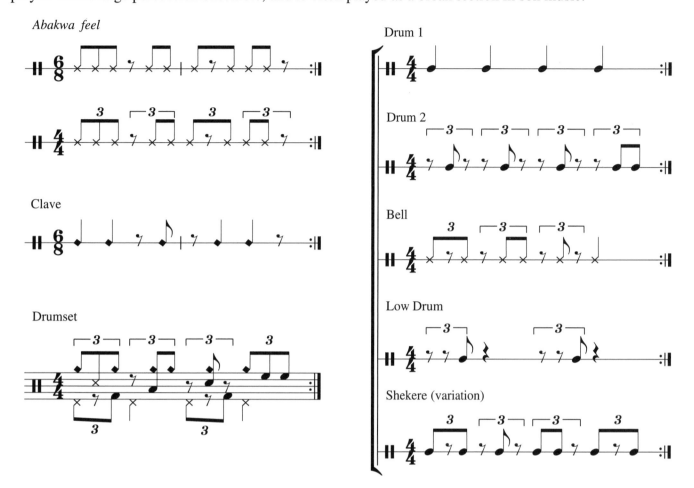

NENGÓN

Nengón originated in Baracoa, a municipality of the Guantánamo province, and is known to be the precursor to both son montuno and changüí. Nengón was traditionally played with a *tingotalango* or *tumbandera* (a bass instrument made with a tree and rope). Nengón is a simple, melodic folk form based on two chords. The singer improvises the verses and alternates with the choruses.

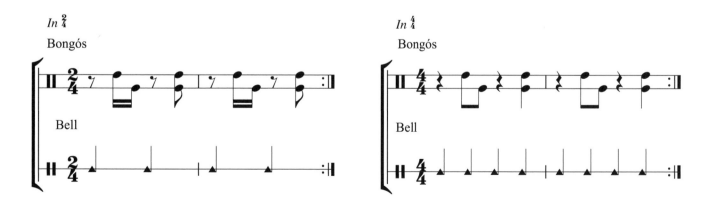

NORTEÑO

Norteño is a combination of Czech and German rhythms that influenced the folk music in the northern region of Mexico. This style is very diverse and has a lot of variations, among the most popular: *ranchera*, *conjunto*, *banda*, *quebradita*, *corrido*, and *tejano*.

PALITO

Palito is the Spanish name for "little stick." This rhythm is the predecessor of the cáscara pattern and was originally played on an instrument called a *gua-gua*, which was a clave-style instrument made of bamboo. This rhythm is emblematic of the rumba style.

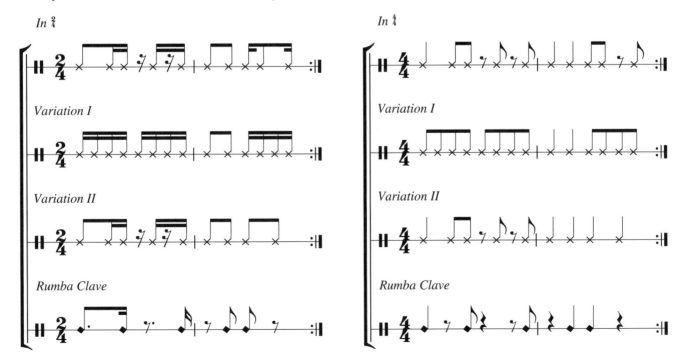

PILÓN

Pilón is a dance based on the motions of pounding sugarcane and was made popular by Enrique Bonne in the 1960s. This rhythm is from the eastern part of Cuba.

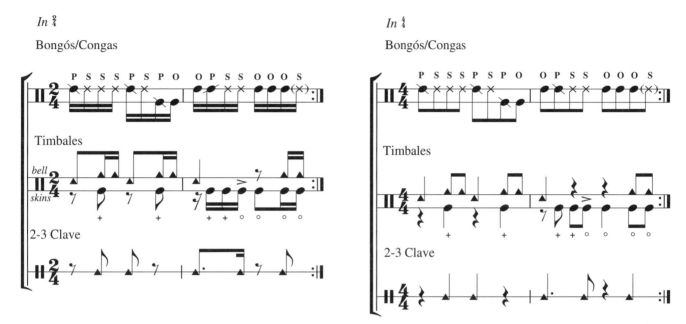

PLENA

Plena is a Puerto Rican rhythm that incorporates African and Spanish elements. Traditional plena is played with a percussion ensemble, *cuatro* (four-stringed folk guitar), and accordion.

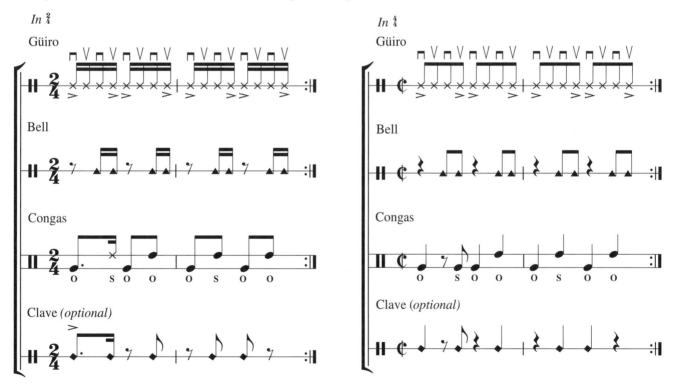

RUMBA

Rumba is an Afro-Cuban style that consists of folk percussion rhythms that accompany singers and dancers. The most popular rumba rhythms are: *guaguancó*, *yambú* and *colombia*.

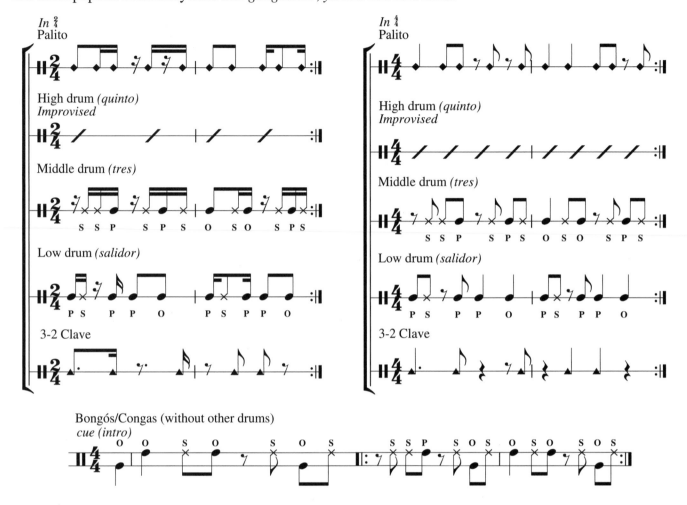

SAMBA

Samba is the most popular Afro-Brazilian rhythm. There are different variations depending on the region, but all of them have their origin in Congolese and Angolan rhythms. The main characteristics of this style are: an accented beat 2; a percussion ensemble of drums, tambourine and cowbells; and $\frac{2}{4}$ meter. Here are some of the most popular sambas from different parts of Brazil:

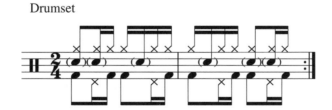

SAMBA · Samba Choro

SAMBA · Samba de portito alto

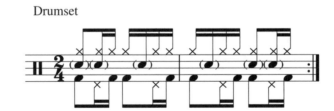

SON

Son is the most influential Cuban style. Started in the second half of the nineteenth century in the eastern province of Oriente, son combines Spanish elements of the *canción* style with African rhythm and percussion. Early forms were interpreted by the *campesinos* (peasants) and developed by the changüí groups.

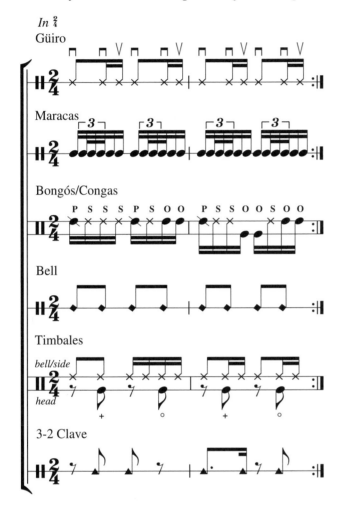

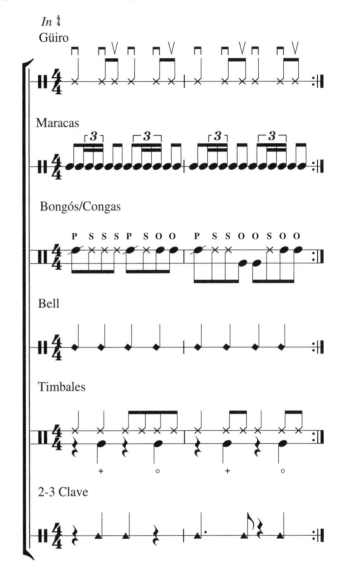

SONGO

Songo is an Afro-Cuban rhythm created by Jose Luis "Changuito" Quintana of Cuba's premiere son group: Los Van Van. This is one of the first Afro-Cuban rhythms created specifically for the drumset.

SUCU-SUCU

Sucu-sucu is a variation of Cuban son. Originally from the Isla de Juventud, sucu-sucu was a party rhythm that eventually became a style of its own. The traditional instrumentation of sucu-sucu is tres, bass (or marímbula), machetes, güiro, maracas, cowbell, bongós and conga.

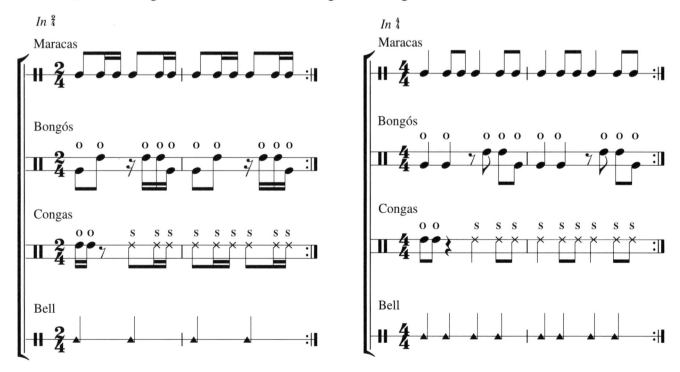

TANGO

Tango is the traditional music and dance of Argentina. Written below for drumset, this nineteenth-century rhythm was originally played with castanets. Tango music is traditionally played by an *orquesta típica*, an ensemble comprised of violin, piano, guitar, flute, and *bandoneón* (a hexagonal chromatic accordion).

VALLENATO

Vallenato is a Colombian folk rhythm very similar to cumbia. Vallenato's main instruments include the *caja* (percussion box), a *guacharaca* (a kind of güiro), and accordion. The emphasis of this rhythm falls on the strong beats.

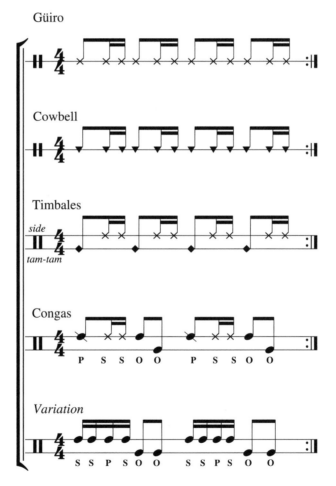

WORLD RHYTHM & PERCUSSION

AFRICA

Due to the immense amount of folk rhythms and the diversity of the ethnical groups and styles of this continent, only the most popular African rhythms are presented here. The following are not Afro-Cuban or strict clave-based rhythms. For more information on those, please refer to the *Latin Rhythm* and *Percussion* section of this book.

ADOWA

Adowa music is originally from Ghana. This music used to be played in funeral processions of the Ashanti people. The main percussion instruments used in this rhythm are: *atumpan* drums and *donno* drums (both talking drums), *petia* drums (medium high-pitched drums), an *apentemma* drum (medium-pitched hand drum), *ntrowas* (rattles), and *dawuros* (African ago-gô bells).

Here is a typical adowa drum rhythm ensemble:

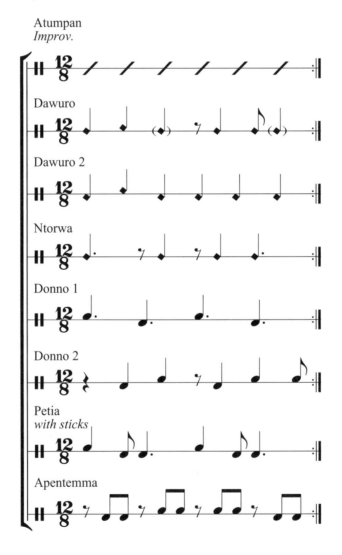

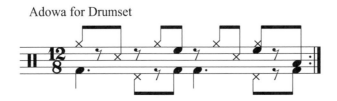

Adowa for Drumset

AKOM

Akom music is played to accompany religious dances of the different religions of West Africa (Ghana). This music tends to be hypnotic and powerful, with different tempos and patterns played at different parts of each ceremony.

The instruments used in these types of rhythms are: the *atumpan* (talking drum), an *opreten* (medium-pitched carved wooden drum), a *dawuro* (African ago-gô bells), an *apentemma* drum (medium-pitched hand drum), and an *agyegyewa* drum (small high-pitched drum).

Here are two of the most common akom rhythms:

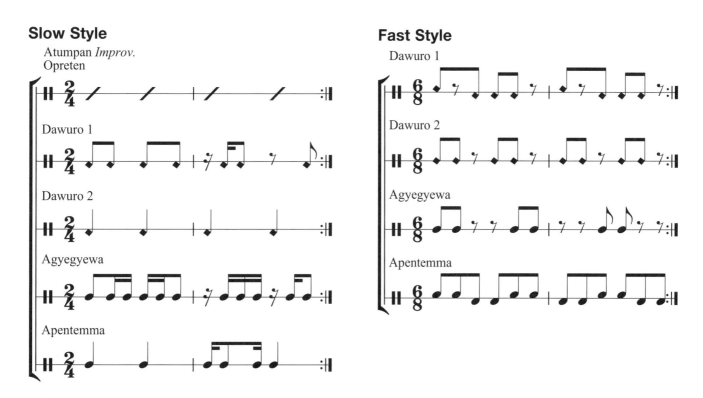

AFROBEAT, AFROPOP AND HIGHLIFE

Afrobeat is a combination of jazz, funk, and African beats. It is believed the Nigerian musician Fela Ransome Anikulapo created this style in the early seventies as a response to the dominating presence of British rock and American soul.

Afropop is the contemporary form of afrobeat, a combination of African and western rhythms—oftentimes called *world beat*. During the seventies and the eighties, African musicians migrated to Europe and to America in order to pursue a professional career. Afropop is the result of mixing traditional African rhythms with western popular music, in many cases, incorporating the new available technology—like synthesizers and guitars—into their styles.

Highlife is the original afropop rhythm. It started in Ghana and Nigeria as ballroom music in the 1920s. This was the first widely popular African dance music known to Europe and America.

The following drumset rhythms are some of the most standard afrobeat/afropop patterns.

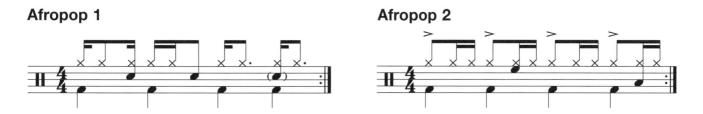

BIKUTSI

Bikutsi is a popular Cameroonian rhythm created as a reaction to the predominant presence of Martinique's *zouk* style (African-influenced jazz), which was the most popular rhythm in the nineties.

Bikutsi is usually played on the drumset, which plays a steady metronome-like rhythm that allows the other percussion instruments (like shakers and drums) to improvise on top of it.

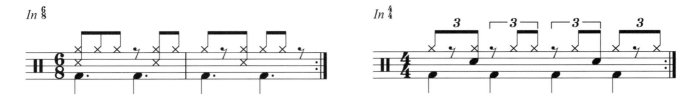

DOUDOUMBA (OR DUNUNBA)

Doudoumba (Guinea, Mali, and Senegal) is also known as "the dance of the strong men." This rhythm is mainly played with *djembes* and *dunduns* (African bass drums played with sticks). There are many variants of the doudoumba rhythm. The original dance is very acrobatic. The dancers, called *barati* (or masters of *bara*, the public place where the doudoumba is performed), show off their vitality and bravery. They strike their bodies with riding crops made from animal muscle while performing risky somersaults and jumps.

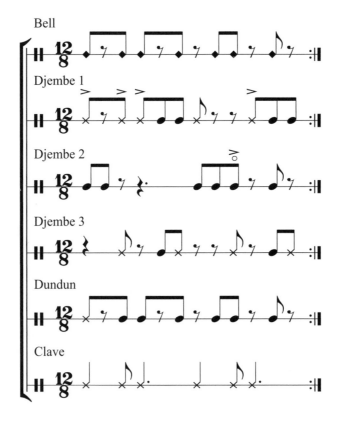

GNAWA (GNAOUA)

Gnawa is a term used to define both African (mainly Moroccan) and Muslim percussion rhythmic traditions, oftentimes involving healing rituals. The word comes from a Saharan Berber dialect's word for "black men" (*aguinaw* or *agenaou*), which was distorted in Western (European) usage to form the word "Guinea."

Gnawa is a very hypnotic, trancelike music characterized by low tones played on the *tbel* (drum); rhythmic melodies played on *gogos* and *guembris* (African lutes); handclapping, and *krakebs* or *karkabous* (metal castanets).

Here are some of the most basic patterns:

Gnawa 1   Gnawa 2

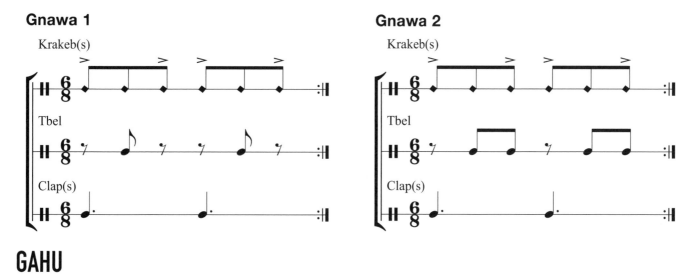

GAHU

Gahu is a very popular dance rhythm among the Ewe (Eve) people of South Ghana, Togo, and Benin.

The main percussion instruments used in this rhythm are carved wooden drums of different diameter sizes: *kaganu* (small), *kidi* (medium), *sogo* (big), and *boba* (the largest). The other instruments played in this rhythm are the *axatse* (gourd shaker) and the *gankogui*, or *gakpevi* (a joint two-hand bell).

Here is one of the most common gahu rhythms:

MAGHREB (RAÏ)

The word *maghreb* means "sunset" in Arabic. This rhythm is the result of the combination of Arabic and African traditions. Maghreb music can be found in Morocco, Western Sahara, Algeria, Tunisia, Mauritania, and Libya. *Raï* is the pop version of maghreb music. Reggae, rock, funk, and ska have all influenced modern raï. This version of maghreb music started in the seventies and is usually played on a drumset. Arab music is still a major influence in this music.

TRADITIONAL MAGHREB

Maghreb is played with instruments that have more resemblance to Middle Eastern percussion than traditional African ones. Some of the most popular maghreb drums are: the *bendir*, a frame drum made from wood and covered with animal skin; the *krakeb* or *kakabou*, two metal beaters shaped like castanets that usually play eighth-note patterns; the *darbuka*, a cone-shaped drum made of clay (traditional) or metal (modern) that can produce a wide variety of pitches both loud and soft; and the *guellal*, a drum made from a piece of piping. The following example is an adaptation of a traditional maghreb pattern.

RAÏ (MODERN MAGHREB)

Raï is played on a regular drumset.

84

SABAR

Sabar (Senegal) is named after the drums used to play it (sabar drums). Sabar music is played for special occasions, celebrations, and festivals. Sabar drumming is also performed for wrestling matches, where each wrestler is given a rhythm of their own. The most accomplished and popular promoter of traditional sabar drumming is *griot* (master drummer) Doudou Ndiaye Rose and his family. The most popular contemporary African artists that incorporate this rhythm into their music are Africando and Youssou N'Dour.

Sabar drums are made of carved wood with goatskin heads. The tuning of the drums is based on a seven-peg system and they are played with a *galan* (stick) and one hand. The traditional sabar drums most often used are: the *m'bung m'bungs* (m'beungbeung), in both small (*m'bung m'bung tungoné*) and large (*m'bung m'bung bal*) sizes; the *sabar n'der* (usually the guide in the ensemble); the *lambe* (or *lamba*), a low-pitched drum; the *talmbat*, a tenor drum; the *gorong yeguel* (created by Doudou Ndiaye Rose), which is similar to the sabar n'der; the *tama* (a talking drum), and the *khine* (or *xeen*), a small sabar drum.

SIKYI

Sikyi is one of the most popular dances of Ghana's Ashanti people. This dance/rhythm is very fast and jolly, usually played as a mating dance.

The main percussion instruments used in this rhythm are: an *oprenten* (the main carved wooden drum), *donno* drums (talking drums), an *agyegyewa* drum (small high-pitched drum), an *apentemma* drum (medium-pitched hand drum), *tamalins* (frame drums), *ntrowas* (rattles), and a *frikyiwa* (metal castanet-type bell).

Here is a typical sikyi rhythm ensemble:

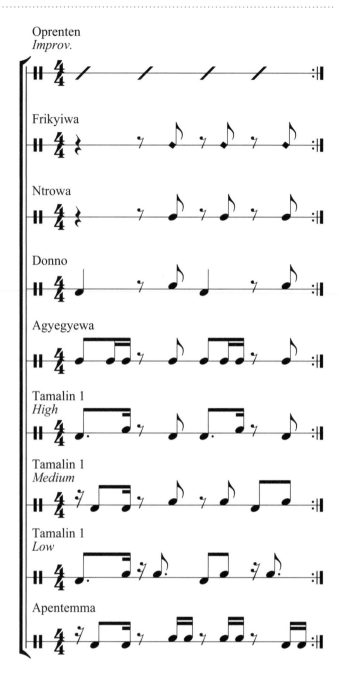

SOUKOUS AND NDOMBOLO

This is one of the most popular music (and dance) styles in all of sub-Saharan Africa. *Soukous* comes from the French word *secouer*, which means "to shake." The rumba music of the fifties and sixties developed into an uptempo rhythm played by some of Africa's best guitarists, eventually giving birth to soukous. Many of Africa's most popular musicians play this style of music, to name a few: Papa Wemba, Tabu Ley Rochereau, Koffi Olomide, Wenga Musica, Soukous Stars, Diblo Dibala, and Kanda Bongo Man. In the mid-nineties, soukous music evolved into a faster-paced new style called *ndombolo*, which remains one of the most popular styles in Africa.

INDIA

The main rhythmic traditions of Indian rhythms can be found in the *Carnatic music* of South India and the *Hindustani music* of North India. The Carnatic music of South India is a complex system that can be traced back to the *Samaveda* tradition. The Hindustani music of North India developed among Hindus and Muslims alike, producing an extremely rich rhythmic system.

SOUTH INDIA · Carnatic Music

The basic rhythmic cycle in Indian classical music is called *tala*. Talas start and finish with the same *sam*, or beat.

Classical Indian music has 108 talas, of which 35 are more commonly used in Carnatic music. The *mridangam* is the most important rhythm instrument in Carnatic music of South India.

Talas are executed with the following hand gestures:

Anudhrutam (or Anudruta) [X]

Anundhrutam lasts one *aksara* (beat) in length, and it is performed with a handclap.

Dhrutam (or Druta) [O]

Dhrutam lasts two aksaras (beats) in length, and is performed by a handclap and a wave in the air.

Laghu [I]

Laghu is a variable gesture, in that it can last three, four, five, seven, or nine aksaras in length. The number next to it indicates the laghu's duration. It is performed by a handclap followed by the corresponding number of finger counts (usually tapped against the other hand). The fingers used to count are (in the following order): the pinky (P), the ring (R), the middle (M), and the index (I) finger, repeated as necessary.

Notation Key

♩ = clap
♩ = wave
P = pinky
R = ring
M = middle
I = index

7 MAIN TALAS	Jathis (Beats per Laghu)				
	Tisra 3	Chaturasra 4	Khanda 5	Misra 7	Sankirna 9
I. Dhruva I O I I	mani I3 O I3 I3	srikara I4 O I4 I4	pramana I5 O I5 I5	purna I7 O I7 I7	bhuvana I9 O I9 I9
II. Matya I O I	sara I3 O I3	sama I4 O I4	udaya I5 O I5	udirna I7 O I7	rava I9 O I9
III. Rupaka O I	chakra O I3	patti O I4	raja O I5	kula O I7	bindu O I9
IV. Triputa I O O	sankha I3 O O	adi I4 O O	dushkara I5 O O	lila I7 O O	bhoga I9 O O
V. Jhampa I X O	kadamba I3 X O	madhura I4 X O	chana I5 X O	sura I7 X O	kara I9 X O
VI. Ata I I O O	gupta I3 I3 O O	lekha I4 I4 O O	vidala I5 I5 O O	loya I7 I7 O O	dhira I9 I9 O O
VII. Eka I	sudha I3	mana I4	rata I5	raga I7	vasnu I9

The following are examples of each of the seven main talas:

Mani
(Tisra Jathi - Dhruva Tala)

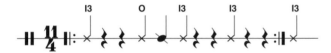

Kara
(Sankirna Jathi - Jhampa Tala)

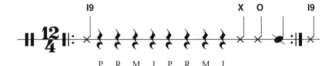

Sama
(Chaturasra Jathi - Matya Tala)

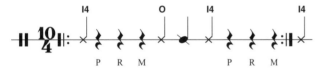

Vidala
(Khanda Jathi - Ata Tala)

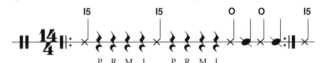

Chakra
(Tisra Jathi - Rupaka Tala)

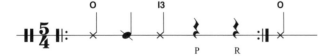

Raga
(Misra Jathi - Eka Tala)

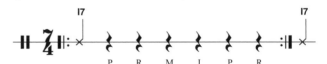

Adi
(Chaturasra Jathi - Triputa Tala)

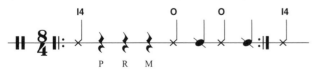

Gatis are smaller subdivisions of the beat (equivalent to Western subdivisions of the beat, i.e., eighth notes, triplets, sixteenth notes, etc.). Gatis are counted with different syllables:

Gati	Divisions per beat	Syllables
tisra gati	3	ta-ki-ta (3)
chaturasra gati	4	ta-ka-di-mi (4)
khanda gati	5	ta-ka-ta-ki-ta (5)
misra gati	7	ta-ki-ta-ta-ka-di-mi (3+4)
sankirna gati	9	ta-ka-di-mi-ta-ka-ta-ki-ta (4+5)

The following example shows Mana Tala (Chaturasra Jathi - Eka Tala) with the practical application of the different gatis.

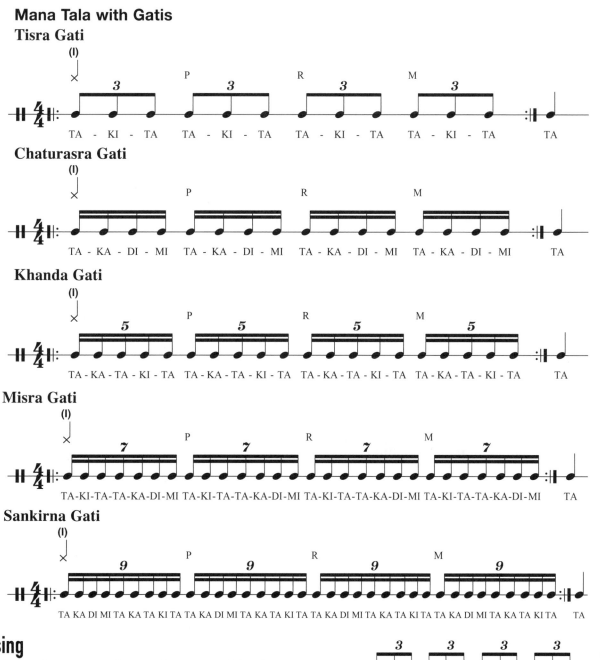

Phrasing

Each of the above examples can be grouped in phrases of three, four, five, seven, or nine. For example, Tisra Gati can be grouped:

The difference between Carnatic and Hindustani music (Hindustani Sangeet or Hindusthani Sangit), is the fact that besides having Hindu musical traditions, Vedic philosophy, and Indian sounds, Hindustani music also has a strong Persian influence from *Afghan Mughals* (Persian empire that ruled parts of modern-day Afghanistan, Baluchistan, and most of the Indian Subcontinent between 1526 and 1707). The most common rhythm instrument in Hindustani music is the *tabla*.

There are approximately 350 Hindustani talas, 10 of which are the most popular and commonly used. These are the basic elements of *kriya*, the time-keeping system in Hindustani music:

Matras: Beats within a *tala* (see *Carnatic music*). There are three kinds of beats:

1. **Sam:** First beat of the tala, the heaviest accent (all variations return to this beat). Represented here by an **X**.

2. **Khali:** A hand wave (see *Carnatic music*) that helps keep and count the time in the tala, represented here by an **O**.

3. **Thali:** Other beats, the accent is not as stressed as it is for a sam. Thalis are represented here by numbers (**2, 3, 4**). Each thali gets a clap. North Indian musicians use claps or hand waves to designate the *vibhags*.

Vibhags: Main subdivisions of the talas, equivalent to the Western music concept of measures.

Bols (derived from the Sanskrit *bolna*, "to speak"): The syllables that correspond to the different tala sounds and strokes.

Theka (meaning "support"): Arrangement of common bols; each tala has one.

The following are some of the most popular talas presented in music notation (*tal lipi*).

Tintal (also called Teental or Trital)

This is the most common tala in Hindustani music. The matras are divided in vibhags of 4 + 4 + 4 + 4.

Keherva (also called Keharwa or Kherva)

This is the most popular non-classical Hindustani tala. The matras are divided in vibhags of 4 + 4.

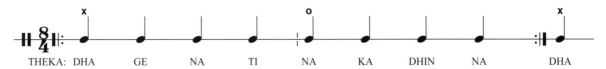

Jhaptal

This is the most popular 10-beat Hindustani tala. The matras are divided in vibhags of 2 + 3 + 2 + 3.

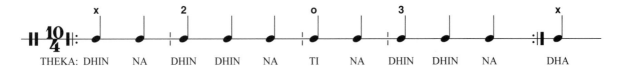

Dadra

This is one of the easiest and most popular 6-beat Hindustani talas. The matras are divided in vibhags of 3 + 3.

THEKA: DHA   DHIN   NA   DHA   TIN   NA   DHA

Chautal (also called Chartal or Chowtal)

This is a very popular tala used in the drupad style (old classical North Indian vocal genre). The matras are divided in vibhags of 4 + 4 + 4 or 4 + 4 + 2 + 2.

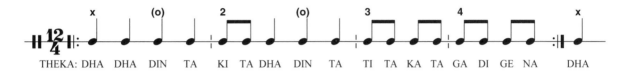

THEKA: DHA DHA DIN TA KI TA DHA DIN TA TI TA KA TA GA DI GE NA   DHA

Rupak (also called Roopak)

This is another common tala used in several Hindustani styles, both classical and popular. This is a very particular tala since the khali (wave) and the sam (strong beat) coincide on the first matra, which makes it start with a wave and not a clap. The matras are divided in vibhags of 3 + 2 + 2.

THEKA: TIN   TIN   NA   DHIN   NA   DHIN   NA   TIN

Ektal

This tala is very popular in *kheyal* (an Indian classical vocal style). The twelve matras that make this tala are divided into six vibhags of two matras each. It can be performed very slow (most common) or relatively fast.

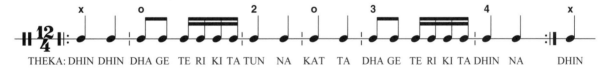

THEKA: DHIN DHIN DHA GE TE RI KI TA TUN NA KAT TA DHA GE TE RI KI TA DHIN NA   DHIN

Dhammar

One of the oldest talas of the classical Hindustani styles. The matras are divided in vibhags of 5 + 2 + 3 + 4.

THEKA: KAT DHE TE DHE TA DHA   GA TE TA TE TA TA   KAT

Tivra

One of the oldest 7-beat talas of the classical Hindustani styles. The matras are divided in vibhags of 3 + 2 + 2.

THEKA: DHA   DIN   TA   TI   TA   KA   TA   GA   DI   GE   NA   DHA

Chachar

This is a very popular tala in North Indian music. The matras are divided in vibhags of 3 + 4 + 3 + 4.

THEKA: DHA   DHIN   DHA   DHA   TI   TA   TI   DHA   DHA   DHI   DHA

IRELAND AND SCOTLAND

CELTIC MUSIC

Celtic is a term usually applied to the music of Ireland and Scotland. Other places that are considered to be part of the Celtic tradition are: Brittany, Cornwall, Isle of Man, Wales, North Umbria, and Galicia. The most popular musical forms labeled as Celtic were common musical styles of many different places in Western Europe.

For the purpose of this book, the two most popular rhythms played on the *bodhrán* are presented.

Bodhrán

This Irish percussion instrument was originally used as a husk sifter, a grain tray, and in street theater performances (such as *mummers* and *wren-boys*), where it was used as a basic rhythm instrument. It was embraced by modern Celtic (mostly Irish) folk musicians during the 1960s, becoming a standard instrument of this type of music. Although the origin of this instrument is not certain, some scholars believe it came from Persia (like many other frame drums), while others believe it to be of African origin.

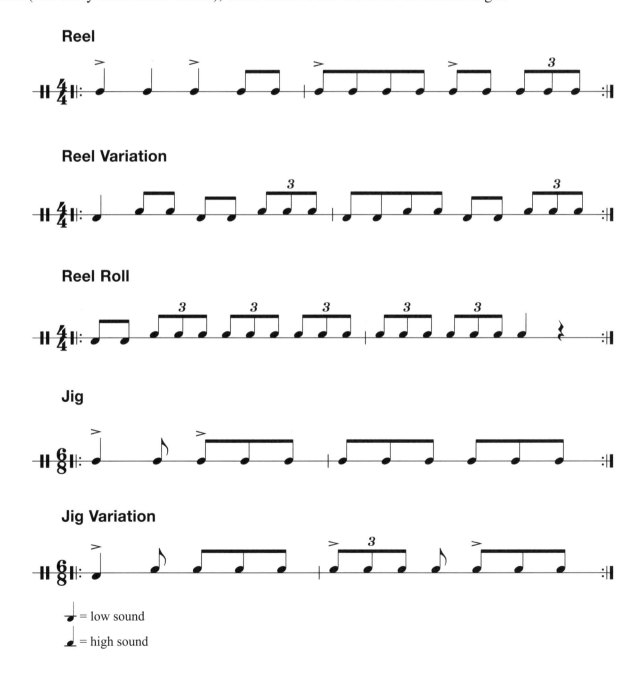

MIDDLE EAST

FRAME DRUM RHYTHMS

Frame drums are some of the oldest percussion instruments on earth. They are made of wood (frame) and thin animal skin (drum head) and sometimes have metal rings (tambourines). Frame drums are typically folk instruments from the Middle East, India, and later, Rome. They were introduced into European society through the influence of Islamic culture. The rhythms presented here are a selection of the most traditional and popular rhythms from the Middle East, as well as related rhythms from the Mediterranean and Balkan regions.

The following drums are used in the performance of these rhythms:

Daf: A traditional *Sufi* instrument in Iran, Kurdistan, Asia, and North Africa. The daf is one of the most popular percussion instruments in Persian (Iranian) music.

Riq: A frame drum used in traditional Arabic music. This frame drum usually has jingles. In contrast to Western musical tradition, this Arabian tambourine is a rather virtuoso instrument.

Darbuka in Turkish; *Dumbek* in Armenian; *Tombak* or *Zarb* in Iran; *Derbekkeh* in Lebanon; *Tarambuke* in the Balkan region, and *Toumbeleki* in Greece: A goblet-shaped drum with a wide range of tones, resonance, and volume. Although not a frame drum per se, it is usually associated with these, since it is used to play the same rhythm patterns.

Frame Drum Notation Key

D *Dum*—open low tone, right hand

T *Tak*—crisp high tone, right hand

K *Ka*—crisp high tone, left hand

P *Pop*—ka while muting the drum with other hand

S *Slap*—closed tone, right hand

G *Grab*—stop, or grab the drum

M *Mute*—left-hand mute dum (low tone)

R *Roll*—finger roll

Maqsum (also Maqsoum or Maqsuum)

Maqsum is the basic and most traditional rhythm throughout the Middle East; it is particularly popular in Egyptian folk music.

Here is a variation with fills:

94

Walking Maqsum

This rhythm is known as "walking" due to the even-sounding strokes produced when playing it.

Baladi (also Balady, Baladii, or Beledi)

Baladi is another Egyptian folk rhythm. Slow in nature, this rhythm is particularly popular when accompanying belly dancers.

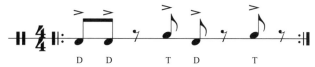

Here is a variation with fills:

Saidi (also Sayyidii or Sa'idi)

This South Egyptian upbeat folk rhythm is played for both traditional (*tahtib*, a men's stick dance) and popular dance (belly dancing) music.

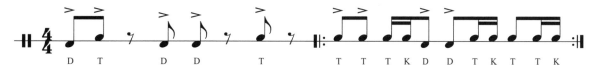

Masmudi (also Masmuudii or Masmoudi)

Another popular belly dancing rhythm, *masmudi* has two joint 4-beat phrases felt in 8. This slow, yet sensual rhythm is commonly played in Morocco as well as Egypt.

Falahi (also Falaahii or Fallahi)

Fallahi is the 2/4 fast version of maqsum.

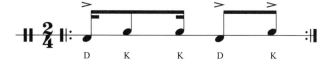

A variation with fills:

Bolero

Middle Eastern *bolero* is a very slow rhythm played in belly dancing. This rhythm was later brought to Spain (and subsequently introduced to Spanish-American colonies such as Cuba), where it was assimilated by the Latin culture and then brought back to influence what we know as modern-day Middle Eastern bolero.

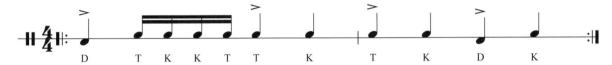

Here is a variation with fills.

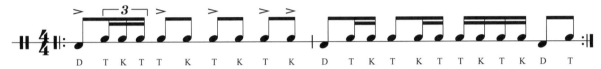

Waahida Taaqasiim (or Waahida Kabiir)

Similar to maqsum, this popular rhythm is usually played at a slow tempo with lots of improvised fills and embellishments. In the Mediterranean region, this rhythm is known as *tsifteteli* or *çiftetelli*.

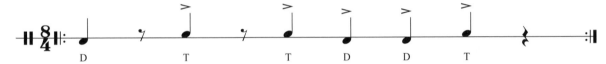

Here is a variation with some fills.

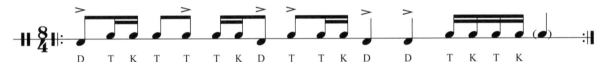

Rumba

Middle Eastern *rumba* is very similar to the Middle Eastern bolero, except it is played twice as fast and in $\frac{2}{4}$.

Here is a variation with some fills.

This is another common variation.

Ayyub or Zaar

Ayyub is commonly used to accompany belly dancing.

Malfuf (or Malfouf), Saudi, and Cosek

This rhythm belongs to the Saudi family of Middle Eastern rhythms. This family consists of rhythms where the accent falls/divides the beats in 3-3-2 patterns. Besides Egypt and Lebanon, the influence of this rhythm can be heard in many popular present-day rhythms such as reggaeton and samba.

D K K T K K T K   D K K T K K T K

Dawr Hindii (Devra Hindi) 3 + 2 + 2

The term *dawr* means that a scale (or rhythm) must return to its starting point (similar to the Carnatic music of India). This rhythm is used in *muwashshat* (a spoken-word Arabic art form).

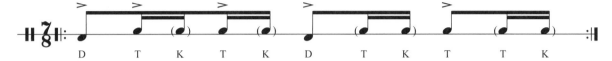

D T K T K D T K T T K

Mediterranean Rhythms

Karsilama (or Antikrystos)

This "face-to-face" (meaning of the word in both Greek and Turkish) 9-beat rhythm is one of the most popular Middle Eastern/Mediterranean compound-meter rhythms. This rhythm is also used to accompany belly dancing, as it can be played fast and slow with different variations.

D   T   D   T T T

Here is a variation with fills.

D K K T K K D K K T T T

Serto

This Greek rhythm shifts the accent from the low to the high tone on every other measure.

D K D K T K D K T K T K

Laz (or Lazs) 2 + 2 + 3

This rhythm is used in different Turkish and Greek folk dances and songs.

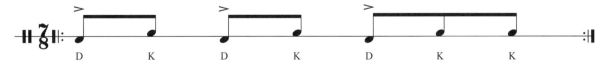

D K D K D K K

Kalamantiano (or Kalamatiano Lazs) 3 + 2 + 2

This is another popular rhythm played to accompany folk tunes and traditional dances. Kalamai (from *kalamata*, meaning "old") is a southern Greek city port on the Mediterranean Sea.

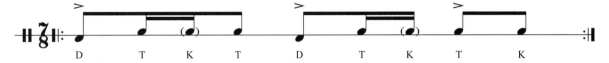

Zeybekiko (Zeymbekiko, Zeybegi, or Zeybek) 4 + 4 + 1

The *Zeybekiko* is an improvisational solo dance from the Mediterranean area. It is a slow fill-free rhythm that accompanies the dance of the same name (danced mainly by men).

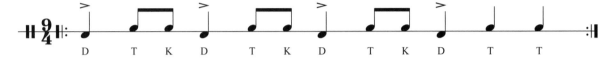

This is another syncopated modern variation:

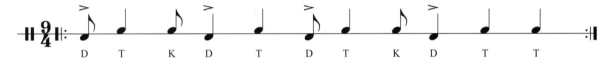

Tsamiko

This is another traditional Greek dance, also danced mostly by men. This dance is performed to celebrate national and folkloric events.

Another variation:

This is a syncopated modern variation.

Persian Rhythms

Usually played on the daf, these are the most popular Iranian traditional rhythms (in their basic forms).

Daem (4)

Garyan (14)

Haddadi (8)

HalGerten

HayAllah (8)

HayAllahAllah (10)

Maddahi (12)

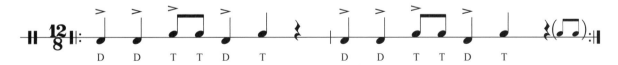

Saghghezi

Zekr-e-Dovvom (16)

SOUTH AMERICA

BERIMBAU (GUNGA) RHYTHMS

Berimbau is an Afro-Brazilian bow-shaped string percussion instrument. Berimbau is intrinsic to the practice and performance of the music that accompanies the martial art dance called *capoeira*.

Berimbau Notation Key

- o *arame* (steel string) low tone
- + arame high tone, while pressing *dobrão* (stone)
- ⬖ *buzz tone* (arame + while lightly touching the dobrão)
- x *caxixi* (small rattle) shake
- ●╱● play first note on arame, damp second note with dobrão

The following patterns (or *toques*) are the most popular rhythms performed with the berimbau.

Toque de Angola

This is the slowest and most common of all of capoeria toques. This toque usually initiates the dance.

    ◣ = close *(cabaça close to body)*
    ◥ = open *(cabaça away from body)*

Toque de São Bento Pequeno

This rhythm is very similar to toque de Angola but much faster, alternating the high and low tones of the arame.

Toque de São Bento Grande (de Angola)

This toque contains the basic capoeira rhythm and has many variations.

Toque de Cavalaria

This toque used to be played to warn capoeiristas when the police were coming. Nowadays, it is used to accompany a fast dance.

Toque de Iúna

This toque is the only rhythm that is played with the berimbau alone. The dance it accompanies is very artistic and acrobatic.

Toque de Santa Maria

This toque is played to accompany the knife dance (dancers attach razors to their feet) or the money dance, where the dancers try to pick up with their mouth a purse full of coins placed in the center of the circle.

Toque de Amazonas

This toque is played to greet visitors.

Toque de Idalina

This is a very slow toque.

TUNING & MAINTAINING YOUR DRUMSET

Tuning

Tuning is the process of producing or preparing to produce a certain pitch in relation to another pitch. Since most percussion instruments are non-pitched, tuning refers to the relative highness or lowness of each instrument and serves to accentuate or diminish certain overtones according to taste.

In order to achieve the correct tuning of a certain group of drums, we must adjust one drum at a time by adjusting the tension on each drum head through the tightening or loosening of the *tuning lugs*.

After tuning one drum (adjusting for overtones and highness or lowness), we can then proceed to correctly tune the rest of the drums in relation to the first. This way, we are using the first drum as our *reference pitch*. The reference pitch for the first drum is typically obtained from a tuning fork, an electronic tuning device, a piano, or an oboe if you are playing in an orchestra.

The Snare Drum

Step 1: Cleaning the Snare Drum

Use a clean, dry cloth to wipe off the hoop (rim) and the shell. Make sure you remove stick shavings, dust, and any buildup that may have accumulated in or around the edges. Clean the inside of the drum as well.

Place the head onto the shell and spin it around the edge to make sure there is nothing in between. Tighten the tension rods until they make contact with the hoop. Do not apply any pressure yet.

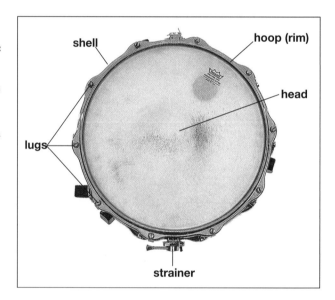

Make sure the snares are turned off. (The snares are a set of curled metal wires located on top of the bottom head.) The snare drum cannot be tuned with interference from the snares.

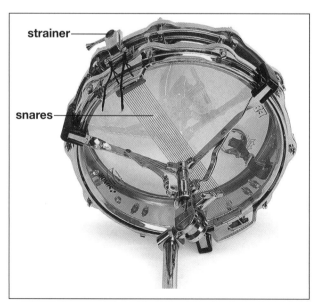

Step 2: Tuning

Always tune the top head first. Place the new head on top of the metal shell and turn each lug clockwise to increase the tension on the head, which raises the pitch of the drum.

The lugs have to be adjusted one at a time, always tuning the next lug located opposite of the first (180° away). By tuning the snare drum in this manner, we achieve uniform tension on all sides of the drum head. This tuning process is known as *opposite-lug sequence.*

The following diagrams show the tightening order for drums with four, six, eight, ten and twelve lugs. Follow these steps in order to achieve an even tension and accurate tuning.

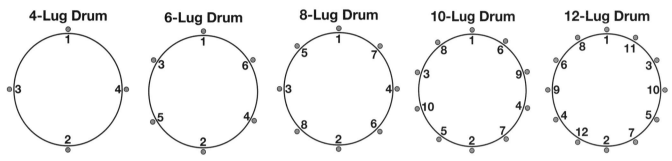

Step 3: Fine-Tuning the Drum Head

Repeat the above tuning process on the bottom head. As you tighten the head, apply smaller increments of pressure (half and quarter turns) to the lugs. Because bottom snare drum heads are thinner and tend to break more easily, be careful not to tune it too high. Tap around the circumference of the head, listening for low-tuned areas. Test the pitch of each lug by lightly tapping about one inch away from the lug with a drumstick (some drummers prefer to use their fingertips). Listen carefully for the high and low spots. Tighten the low areas in order to achieve consistency. Try detuning each lug and then slowly tune it up again to try to match the pitches.

Snare Drum Tuning Tips

When tuning the snare drum, remember that the tighter the bottom head, the more the snares will vibrate, producing a drier sound. The looser the bottom head, the less the snares will vibrate. As a result, the drum will produce a loose, "fluffy" sound.

The vibration of the snares against the bottom drum head can also be adjusted by the tightness of the *strainer*, which is usually located on the side of the snare's shell. The tighter the strainer, the shorter the duration of the buzz; the looser the strainer, the longer the duration of the buzz.

Tune the bottom head to get a snare sound that will best accommodate your individual style of music. Some styles require a tighter sound, while others sound best with a loose buzz.

The Bass Drum

Step 1: Tuning the Front Head

The front head should always be tuned first. Since the tightness of this head doesn't greatly affect the overall sound of the bass drum, some drummers choose to tighten it just enough so it doesn't look wrinkled.

Step 2: Tuning the Back Head

Follow **Step 2** of the snare drum (opposite-lug) tuning sequence. The bass drum should not be tuned so high that it loses its characteristic deep, booming sound. Remember that before the electric bass was invented, the bass drum was used as the foundation of the low frequencies in the rhythm section. The bass drum sound should be appropriate for the style of music you are playing.

Bass Drum Tuning Tips

Test the pitch of the bass drum head with the bass drum pedal only. Smaller beaters or drum sticks can leave undesired marks that can alter the overall bass drum head performance. When tuning the bass drum, make sure that only the felt beater is hitting the head. Any other part of the pedal can easily break the head.

A small hole cut in the front head will let air escape after the head is struck. By doing this, the foot pedal is allowed to bounce at just the right amount. Otherwise, the pedal can bounce too much, resulting in unwanted double notes.

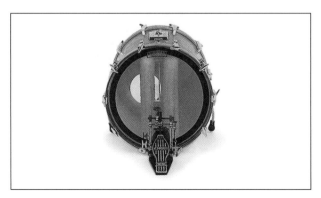

Adjust the internal damping by adding muffling material to the inside of the shell (see **Muffling**). In addition to regulating air pressure, a small hole in your bass drum's front head will allow you to add or modify the amount of muffling material without having to open the bass drum each time.

The Toms

Step 1: Tuning the Bottom Head

Tune the bottom head of each tom first, following **Step 2** of the snare drum (opposite lug) tuning sequence.

Step 2: Tuning the Top Head

After tuning the bottom head, proceed to the top head. At this point, it is very important that you tune the toms in relation to the snare drum. Check the pitch of each tom so that the sound is consistent throughout. Follow **Step 3: Fine-Tuning the Drum Head** of the snare drum tuning section.

GENERAL GUIDELINES FOR DRUMSET TUNING

Pitch

There are three main ways of tuning any two-headed drum (with the exception of the bass drum):

1. *Top and bottom heads at same pitch*
   This tuning gets the sound preferred by most drummers—a warm, invariable sound with lots of sustain and overtones.

2. *Top head tuned at higher pitch*
   This tuning produces a deep sound with a constant pitch and few overtones.

3. *Bottom head tuned at higher pitch*
   This tuning produces a rich and piercing sound that is full of sustain and not too many overtones.

NOTE: The two heads should be tuned only slightly apart. If the heads are tuned too far apart, the sound waves produced by both heads will cancel each other out, resulting in a "dead" snare or tom sound.

Muffling

Muffling can be used to eliminate unwanted overtones and to further customize the sound of your drums.

The most common (and cheapest) method for getting rid of extra overtones is to tape a small piece of tissue to the edge of the drum head. You can also cut rings from old heads and tape them on top of the new heads. Alternate damping material, such as foam rings, cotton, napkins, felt, etc., to achieve different sounds. If you use many mufflers, tape the desired material to the inside of the head so it does not obstruct your playing surface.

If your intention is to get a deeper, "dead" drum sound, apply more material on top of the heads (some drummers even cover the whole drumset). Any type of fabric works well for this particular purpose. The amount of material you use depends on how muted you want your drums to sound.

Plastic and Acrylic Parts

Drum shells are generally made of wood, and are usually coated with some sort of plastic or lacquered finish. The best thing to clean these types of surfaces is mild hand soap and warm water. Glass cleaners and other ammonia-based products will leave the surface dry and dull.

Never use anything abrasive, such as scouring pads or steel wool. They will ruin the plastic finish and scratch the surface.

To add shine to the shells, use furniture polish or guitar polish. Drum manufacturers also make special polishing products.

Always transport your gear in proper cases to protect them from damage. Hardshell cases are the best, since they offer the most protection and will keep your equipment in mint condition the longest.

Metal Parts and Shells

Most, if not all of the hardware in your kit will be chrome plated (or some other variety of metal alloy—see your owner's manual). This chrome coating can easily be ruined. The best way to prevent rusting is to keep your drums dry and dust-free at all times (so avoid storing them in the basement).

After every use, make sure there is not any kind of moisture left on the metal surfaces (such as sweat, condensation, etc.). Always use a soft, dry cloth to prevent scratches.

Wipe down your equipment at least once a week. This will help prevent the formation of rust and the buildup of dust particles. If you see rust, use a commercial rust remover immediately. The longer you wait, the more damage the rust will do to the surface. For severely rusted equipment, some recommend the use of tougher solvents like gasoline or Naptha. You can also try using commercial metal polish for any metal part (other than cymbals). For the special care of cymbals, see **Cymbals**.

Lugs

Dryness and rusting makes lugs stiff and difficult to move. If your lugs have seized, apply small amounts of petroleum jelly (or commercial sewing machine lubricant) into the lugs to free them. Apply the lubricant with a cotton swab or a toothpick and gently screw the tension rod in and take out the lug. Never use a silicone-based lubricant such as WD-40, as it will remove the old lubricant and dry up the lug faster.

Cymbals

This is probably the most difficult and delicate part of the cleaning process. Cleaning and polishing your cymbals is all a matter of personal preference. Some drummers like to clean their cymbals regularly to keep them sounding bright and new. Others choose not to clean their cymbals, since they prefer a darker sound, and argue that cleaning the cymbal damages it since the polish removes metal. In reality, the amount of metal removed is minimal and not significant enough to damage the overall sound of the cymbal.

Use the brand of polish recommended by the manufacturer when cleaning your cymbals, as the materials, coatings, and finishes vary from one manufacturer to another. The recommended polish for one type of cymbal may damage or even ruin another, so always consult your owner's manual.

First, wipe off any loose dirt or dust with a commercial window cleaner. Use two clean cloths—one to apply the product and one to remove it.

Next, apply the correct polish carefully; most cymbal cleaners will remove the cymbal's logo if you wipe over them. Follow your cleaner's directions carefully, and apply small portions in a circular motion.

Clean off any excess polish with a commercial window cleaner, and buff with a soft, dry cloth.

Additional Tips

Car wax can be used to get rid of fingerprints. Apply small amounts of wax in a circular motion (following the cymbal's grooves), letting it dry to form a thin layer or haze. Buff with a dry cloth.

Always clean your cymbals after playing and before storing them. Carry your cymbals in a special hardshell case or cymbal bag. Do not let the cymbals touch each other during travel because friction between the surfaces could damage them.

TUNING & MAINTAINING YOUR PERCUSSION INSTRUMENTS

Tuning is the process of producing or preparing to produce a certain pitch in relation to another pitch. Since most percussion instruments are non-pitched, tuning refers to the relative highness or lowness of each instrument and serves to accentuate or diminish certain overtones according to taste.

Congas

There are no standard pitches for these instruments. The tuning process for these drums is usually set by style, genre, and tradition. *Congeros* (conga players) train their ears over time to know what kind of sound they want out of their instruments.

The most common tunings for these instruments are done with approximate pitch intervals of thirds, fourths (most popular), and fifths.

Step 1: Cleaning and Preparation

Remove the old skin from the conga and clean the edge of the shell thoroughly (household window cleaner works great). If you notice any defects in the shell, such as cracks, splinters, unevenness, etc., take the drum to your local drum technician for repair. Avoid trying to repair the drum yourself; if you do not know how to fix it properly, you could completely ruin the drum. The process is very detailed since the drum needs to be calibrated, sealed, and braced.

Step 2: New Skins (Drum Heads)

Make sure that the skin is dry, flat, relatively soft (depending on the make), and that it is not damaged. The new skin should encircle both the wooden shell and the metal hoop. Place the skin on top of the shell, then place the hoop on top of the skin.

Tighten each tension rod/claw manually until you feel the tension is even in all of the rods. The lugs have to be adjusted one at a time, always tuning the next lug located opposite of the first (180° away). By tuning in this manner, we achieve uniform tension on all sides of the drum head. This tuning process is known as *opposite-lug sequence*.

Step 3: Fine Tuning

Play the head with all the different types of techniques (palm, hand, slaps, open- and closed-tone strokes, finger strokes, etc.) and fine-tune using the opposite-lug tuning sequence. Strive for a warm, deep, and clear conga sound.

Conga Tuning Tips

When tuning your congas, make sure you obtain a pitch that has plenty of sustain when hitting it with an open stroke. This will help reduce undesired overtones.

If you play with two or more congas, try tuning them in thirds, fourths, or fifths for melodic and harmonic consistency.

Tune the congas slowly so that you can notice the differences in tone. Again, try all kinds of strokes with each tuning increment.

When finished playing, tune your congas down a considerable amount. This will extend the life of your heads and will help to fine-tune your ears. This will also allow you to experiment with different tunings each time you play.

Change your heads when the sound of your drums becomes dull, before a recording session, or every few months if you are playing frequently.

Bongós

Just like congas, there are not any standard pitches for this instrument. *Bongoceros* (bongo players) tune by ear according to style, genre, and tradition.

Bongós are commonly tuned to the approximate pitch intervals of fourths, fifths (most popular), and octaves.

Step 1: Choosing the Right Head

There are several varieties of skins (heads) to choose from:

Hand Tuck Natural (flat) Skins. These skins need to be hand-tucked. In order to use and tune these types of skins, you need to wet the skin to soften it, and then mount it into the bongos. When purchasing these types of heads, check that both the surface and the thickness of the skins are even.

Mountable Natural (rawhide) Skins. These skins are the most popular since they are already sized and fitted, ready to mount and tune.

Mountable Synthetic Skins. These heads are usually made of a variety of flexible plastic materials. Because they can be tuned higher, these skins will make your bongos sound brighter and louder.

Step 2: Tuning the Heads

Refer to **Steps 2** and **3** of the conga tuning section for specific instructions. If you are using natural skins, make sure that the skins are dry before starting the opposite-lug sequence. Some people like to tune in a clockwise direction, but the opposite-lug sequence distributes the tension in a more even manner, thus helping you achieve a more accurate tuning.

The *macho* (smaller) drum head must be tuned very tightly in order to get a sharp and crisp open tone. The *hembra* (larger) drum must be tuned at a lower pitch, such as a fifth or an octave below the *macho*.

Bongó Tuning Tips

Apply lug oil before reinserting the tuning lugs. This will make the tuning process easier and prevent the lugs from seizing.

Tighten the head as much as needed. Well-tuned bongós produce a nicer tone than loosely tuned ones.

Weather will most certainly affect the tuning of natural skins. The pitch will rise in warm weather and drop in cold weather. Always make sure that your tuning is correct before you start playing or recording.

Detune your drums after playing. This will extend the life of your heads and fine-tune your ear. This will also allow you to experiment with different tunings every time you play.

It is not necessary to detune synthetic heads, but this is still a good procedure to follow since detuning also keeps tension off the drum shell.

Change your heads when the sound of your instrument is not as bright, before recording, or every few months if you are playing often.

GLOSSARY

Abakwa (Abacuá or Abakuá). This rhythm was developed by a secret fraternal society of the African Carabalí people in Cuba. This musical style influenced other popular genres such as the rumba and guaguancó.

Afoxé. 1. Religious music from the Yoruba tribe. 2. A *cabasa* (squash or pumpkin) covered with a net of shells that is used as a shaker.

Ago-gô. A double bell played with a stick or metal beater. The shape of this bell is triangular (conical), connected by a piece of bent metal, and tuned a relative fourth (or sometimes a fifth) apart. Some ago-gôs are made of three or more bells with different tunings.

Apanpichao. Third (or swing) section of the merengue rhythm.

Banda. A traditional Mexican brass ensemble musical form, banda became popular around the 1960s in Sinaloa, Mexico. It achieved its peak popularity in the late 1990s throughout Mexico and in the southwest United States—especially in Texas, California and, to a lesser degree, in Iowa, Kansas, and Illinois.

Batucada. Samba played by percussion instruments only. Batucada is loud and energetic, and usually played by a large street-samba ensemble.

Bembé. 1. Popular Afro-Cuban § rhythm. Bembé(s) is the African word used for religious gatherings that include drumming, singing and dancing in honor of Orisha. 2. Traditional drums made from hollowed palm tree logs with nailed-on skins tuned with heat and used in the bembé ceremonies.

Bolero (Cuban). Afro-Cuban ballad with a moderate-slow tempo in which the lyric content is mostly romantic. Pepe Sánchez has been credited with creating the Cuban bolero in 1885 with a composition called "Tristeza."

Bomba. 1. Puerto Rican folk musical form and dance with African influence. 2. Large barrel-shaped drums similar to, but smaller than, the tumbadora, used to play the bomba rhythm.

Cajón. Box made from wood used in Cuban and Spanish music as a percussion instrument.

Canção. Portuguese for "song."

Canción. Spanish for "song."

Candomblé. A religion that came to Brazil from Africa. The name *Batuque* is also used, especially before the nineteenth century when candomblé became more common. Both words are believed to derive from a Bantu-family language.

Cavaquinho. Small Brazilian guitar made of four metal strings.

Caxixi. Conical-shaped shaker built of basketwork material.

Charanga. Cuban orchestra usually comprised of piano, strings, vocals and percussion. The term also describes a style with the above-mentioned orchestration.

Clave. Rhythmic pattern that is the foundation of most traditional Cuban music.

Claves. Percussion instrument made of two wooden sticks that are used to play the clave rhythm.

Columbia. Rumba style played in § and sung with a combination of Spanish and African phrases.

Comparsa. A Cuban party or dance that includes music and dancing, or the band that plays during the celebration.

Congas. Medium-to large-sized drums of Congolese origin (*makuta* drums) used for most Latin-American folk music. The most popular sizes are: the *niño* (25 cm), the *quinto* (28 cm), the *conga*, *seguidor* or *tres golpes* (30 cm), and the *tumbadora* (term used in Cuba) or *salidor* (33 cm). Congas are now very common in Latin music.

Conjunto. Traditional Mexican musical style originated in rural northern Mexico in the early twentieth century. This music is based largely on *corridos* and polka. Conjunto and norteño are interchangeable terms used to describe the same style.

Corrido. Narrative song and poetry form of the northern Mexican states that became the most popular style during the Mexican revolution in the early part of the twentieth century. The traditional corrido has a political tone.

Cuatro. A Latin-American guitar-like instrument. The most popular *cuatros* are from Puerto Rico and Venezuela. There are three main types of Puerto Rican cuatros: *Cuatro antigüo* of 4 orders and 4 strings, *Southern cuatro* of 4 orders and 8 strings, and *Cuatro moderno* of 5 orders and 10 strings. The cuatro of Venezuela has four single strings.

Cuica. Brazilian single-headed drum with a rod connected to the underside of the drum head. The rod is pulled with a wet cloth, which creates friction and produces the characteristic sound of the instrument.

Four on the floor. Popular drummer's term that refers to playing four quarter notes on the bass drum consequently and throughout any given rhythm (usually in $\frac{4}{4}$ meter).

Ganzá. Brazilian percussion instrument (shaker) of cylindrical shape filled with stones or pieces of metal.

Gua-gua. Bamboo piece that is mounted and used to play palito patterns.

Guaguancó. An Afro-Cuban music and dance that is a subgenre of the rumba. The dance is traditionally performed by a male and female duo. The male depicts the attempted sexual "capture" of the female by a pelvic thrust called the *Vacunáo*.

Güiro. Latin percussion instrument made of a calabash gourd with ridges carved in the skin.

Jaleo. Second section of the merengue rhythm.

Maracas. Hand-held, canister-like rattles with handles played in pairs. Originally made from gourds or dried rawhide and filled with materials such as beads, pebbles and seeds.

Pandeiro. Brazilian tambourine with jingles.

Quebradita. Fast-tempo subgenre of norteño music often performed by a large brass ensemble, vocalists, and percussion.

Quinto. See *congas*.

Ranchera. Slow tempo song subgenre of norteño music. Ranchera instrumentation is usually minimal (e.g., solo guitar).

Repinique (or repique). Brazilian double-headed drum carried over the shoulders, which usually cues the other players.

Salidor. See *congas*.

Salsa. Generic term developed in the late sixties–early seventies used to describe the blending of numerous specific Latin styles into dance orchestra arrangements. The common element in the musical structure is the rhythm pattern of the clave. The word *salsa* means "sauce" in Spanish.

Samba de partido alto (or *Samba de cidade*, **"city samba").** In this type of samba, a lead singer improvises verses that alternate with the chorus. The most characteristic feature of this samba is the pandeiro rhythm.

Samba de salão. This saloon *(salão)* samba has a lighter feel than that of *partido alto* and is usually performed with a small ensemble.

Samba-choro. This samba dates to the early nineteenth century. Choro is light music, and often has breaks. The A-B musical form is characteristic of this style.

Shekere. African percussion instrument made of a gourd covered with a net of beads (or shells).

Surdo. Brazilian double-headed bass drum. Compared to the zambumba, the surdo is taller.

Tambora. Double-headed drum from the Dominican Republic used in the merengue rhythm. The drum is played with a stick that strikes one head and the wooden shell of the drum, while the hand plays the opposite head.

Tamborim. Brazilian small frame drum played with a stick.

Tejano. The term used in Spanish for "Texan." This style is a combination of various forms of traditional and popular Mexican music with rock, cumbia, and blues, and was created by the descendants of Mexican immigrants in Texas *(Tejanos)*. Tex-Mex refers to the more traditional styles such as norteño music. Tejano is usually more modern and is heavily influenced by contemporary popular styles.

Timbal(es). Cuban drums mounted on a stand and played with drumsticks. Measuring in sizes from 13 to 15 inches in diameter, they usually come in pairs, either 13 and 14, or 14 and 15 inches. This instrument is very characteristic of danzón music.

Tres. Small guitar-like instrument, originally from Cuba. The tres can have either three sets of two strings or three sets of three strings. This instrument is highly characteristic of the changüí and son (traditional) styles.

Tres golpes. See *congas*.

Yambú. A type of rumba traditionally performed on the cajón. Yambú is danced by a male-female duo in a slow to medium tempo in duple meter.

Zabumba. Flat, double-headed bass drum originally from Brazil.